CULTURAL MEMORY AND BIODIVERSITY

CULTURAL MEMORY AND BIODIVERSITY

VIRGINIA D. NAZAREA

THE UNIVERSITY
OF ARIZONA PRESS
TUCSON

Publication of this book is made possible in part by a grant from the Centro Internacional de la Papa.

The University of Arizona Press
© 1998 The Arizona Board of Regents
First Printing

∞This book is printed on acid-free, archival-quality paper.
Manufactured in the United States of America

03   02   01 . 00   99   98   6   5   4   3   2   1

Library of Congress Cataloging-in-Publication Data

Nazarea, Virginia D. (Virginia Dimasuay), 1954–
Cultural memory and biodiversity / Virginia D. Nazarea.
p.   cm.
Includes biblographical references and index.
ISBN 0-8165-1681-2 (cloth : acid-free paper)
1. Ethnobiology.   2. Germplasm resources, Plant—Collection and preservation.   3. Traditional farming.   4. Plants, Cultivated—Germplasm resources.   5. Gene banks, plant.   6. Soil seed banks.
7. Human ecology.   I. Title.
GN476.N39 1998   97-45265
306.4′5—dc21   CIP

British Library Cataloguing-in-Publication Data
A catalogue record for this book is available from the British Library.

CONTENTS

FIGURES

TABLES

PREFACE

In a novel entitled *Noli Me Tangere* (Touch Me Not) that Jose Rizal wrote to expose Spanish abuses in the Philippines during the eighteenth century, he painted an interesting character, Pilosopong Tacio. *Pilosopo* has a multilayered meaning in Pilipino. On one hand, it denotes and directly translates as philosopher, sage, wise man. On the other hand, it connotes someone who consistently challenges conventions or someone who perhaps is not quite socialized to know the cultural rules, someone who "marches to the beat of a different drummer" and thus is always a thorn in the side of established order. There is at least one in every village.

In Kabaritan, where I once did fieldwork in a lowland, irrigated rice farming community (Nazarea-Sandoval 1995), I met someone whom I will name for now, borrowing from Jose Rizal, Pilosopong Tacio. He lamented the loss of traditional rice varieties that were delicious, aromatic, and "slippery," that did not, according to his folks, demand weeding and irrigation, chemical fertilizers and insecticides, varieties that his wife could use to prepare local delicacies—sticky or light-textured rice cakes, rolls, and porridge.

He told me that he mostly planted high-yielding modern varieties in his farm because, first of all, he did not know where to get seeds for the more favored rices, and second of all, if he alone planted the aromatic varieties, would not all the birds and rats in Kabaritan flock to his fields because they prefer these varieties too? He also revealed that he followed most of the prescriptions of the extension agent regarding his farm but did not exactly understand all that was needed in terms of fertilizing, weeding, and pest control. He shrugged his shoulders, philosophically, and added, "You know, those who know more find pleasure in making things more and more difficult for us who know less."

I wanted to assure my friend that what he knew was not any *less*, it was *different*, and probably in his situation *better*. Yet he and others like him will always think that their knowledge is not on a par with the more technical expertise of the extension agent. On second thought, if I know Pilosopong Tacio, even his comment probably had another, deeper layer of meaning. This was his "public script" (Scott 1990)—spoken tongue-in-cheek—meant to placate but also to probe the forces in a scheme of things he had little control over. His remark was meant to create an impression, trusting me to sort out, at the same time, "what the jest is worth." In a small farm near Pilosopong Tacio's property, his neighbor was planting the recommended green-stalked, high-yielding variety (on which his creditworthiness in large part depended), but cleverly hidden in the middle of every clump, unknown to bank officials and extension agents, who rarely got their feet wet in the rice paddies, were the purple-stalked fragrant varieties that his neighbor desired.

Memory banking addresses the cultural dimensions of biodiversity. It is meant to "capture" memories in a way that runs parallel to, and thereby complements, the preservation and documentation of landraces, wild relatives, and other crop cultivars in germplasm conservation centers around the world. Focusing, in the present work, on a less glamorous and often neglected aspect of biodiversity—the genetic diversity of agricultural crops—it hopes to call attention to the role of local cultures in nurturing and conserving an important component of plant genetic resources. Furthermore, it aims to flesh out the passport data routinely collected for accessions in gene banks with cultural information derived from farmers' oral histories, evaluation criteria, ranking and sorting schema, and cognitive drawings. Lest "capture" be construed in its most sinister hue, let me quickly add that the ultimate goal is for the local population to control access to this knowledge and, at some point, to enable them to derive compensation for its use. I discuss this aspect in greater detail in the final chapter.

The goal of memory banking is to systematically document the knowledge of Pilosopong Tacio and others like him to make sure that this knowledge won't disappear like the rice and other crop varieties that they appreciate, so that the legacy will be preserved for their children and ours should there be a need or an urge to explore options away from the beaten path of high-technology, input-dependent, and narrow-genetic-base agriculture. This book explores the interface between genetic diversity and cultural diversity, in both its robustness and fragility.

There is a Pilosopong Tacio in every village. In Intavas, a subsistence sweet potato production area in Bukidnon, Philippines, Pilosopong Tacio was a woman farmer who tended her sweet potatoes in clumps, expertly choosing whichever variety she liked for her grandchildren's snacks, as a substitute for rice during lean times, for leaves to make into a salad, for medicine to soothe itchy skin, and so on. In Salvacion, a commercial-growing area, Pilosopong Tacio took the form of a market-oriented farmer who nonetheless experimented with as many sweet potato varieties as he could because he realized there was no way he could control market demand, the incidence of pests, the vagaries of weather, or the idiosyncrasies of the land.

My gratitude goes to the farmers of Bukidnon who patiently put up with us as we asked them to rank and sort, draw their varieties from memory, and relate their life stories. Learning from their experiences was a constant source of surprise and enjoyment. They made me realize that marginality imbues certain advantages in the long term—a spirited independence, an insatiable curiosity, an unrelenting innovativeness, and a philosophical irreverence to the lures and threats of the hegemony of modern agriculture—that allow them to nurture both cultural and genetic diversity. Toward the end of the project, they assumed an increasingly active role in the effort and took the initiative of explaining to their neighbors why the undertaking was worth their time and energy. They have given us their blessings and encouragement in sharing the findings of this research with a larger audience and crediting them for their experiences and insights.

I wish to thank colleagues who encouraged me in this endeavor, particularly Duncan Vaughn of the International Rice Germplasm Center; Enrique Chujoy, Gordon Prain, and Hubert Zandstra of the International Potato Center; Pablo Eyzaguire, Masa Iwanaga, and Geoffrey Hawtin of the International Plant Genetic Resources Institute; Joachim Voss of the International Development and Research Council; Michael Soulé of the University of California, Santa Cruz; Harold Conklin of Yale University; and Richard Ford of the University of Michigan. Robert Rhoades, then coordinator of UPWARD (User's Perspective With Agricultural Research and Development), was the first to recognize the merit and feasibility of my memory banking proposal and has not since allowed me to forget.

UPWARD at the International Potato Center in Los Baños, Philippines, was my home while I was doing my memory banking research. The International Potato Center has continued to make memory banking one of its priorities and has partially supported the publication of this book. Philosophically, intellectually, and in other important aspects, UPWARD will always be associated with this project in my mind and heart. At UPWARD, I drew heavily on the friendship and support of the staff and particularly on the assistance of Maricel Piniero, who has been an integral part of this project from day one. She took on this project as her own and continues to give it her very best.

Thanks are also due to my colleagues and students at the University of California, Santa Cruz, and the University of Georgia, Athens. In particular, my appreciation goes to LaBau Bryan for her bottomless good cheer while processing this manuscript, and Eleanor Tison, Joanne Goodwin, and Gabriella Flora for enthusiastic feedback and assistance at various stages of preparation. The Sustainable Agriculture and Natural Resource Management Collaborative Research Support Program (SANREM CRSP) at the University of Georgia supported critical stages of data analysis and text preparation and the creation of the Memory Web.

Memories are memories are memories, and these particular ones are dedicated to my parents, Teofila Dimasuay-Nazarea and Emeterio Toga Nazarea, for being what they are. They taught me a lot of things, and this book is a small acknowledgment of how lucky I am for all that they have shared.

CULTURAL MEMORY AND BIODIVERSITY

1

OF MEMORIES AND VARIETIES

Complementation between Cultural and Genetic Diversity

Conventional agricultural research and extension is part and parcel of "development from above" or, to put it somewhat differently, "development from outside." Implicit in these efforts to modernize the traditional farmer and introduce new agricultural "packages" is the assumption that what is being introduced, by virtue of its being more "scientific" and "advanced," is necessarily superior to varieties and agricultural practices that have evolved in situ. Currently, a small but growing group of researchers and practitioners are pursuing the opposite tack. Indigenous knowledge and the practices of local farmers are being investigated in the hope that they may reveal ideas that contain "seeds" of adaptive value (Alcorn 1984; Hunn 1985; Richards 1985; Rhoades 1994).

Toward this end, Gregory Knight (1980), among others, has called for the systematic documentation of traditional farmers' knowledge into an "information bank" from which agronomists, extension workers, and other farmers can draw enlightenment and insight. This is not to argue that local beliefs are always objective or correct. Nonetheless, such repositories of farmers' traditional knowledge would be a useful antidote for the posture, much resented by local people, of pouring agricultural "know-how" into what are presumed to be empty vessels. Justifiably, farmers consider this arrogance an insult, particularly in relation to the management of biological resources. As Oldfield and Alcorn pointed out, "Much of the world's biological diversity is in the custody of farmers who follow age-old farming and land use practices. These ecologically complex agricultural systems associated with centers of crop genetic diversity include not only the traditional cultivars or 'land races' that constitute an essential part of our world crop genetic heritage, but also wild plant and animal species that serve humanity as biological resources" (1991:37).

In a pioneering and classic study among the Hanunoo of Mindoro, Philippines, Harold Conklin (1954) documented a fine-grained classificatory system that distinguished among 1,600 plant types, including 430 cultivars. Likewise, Brent Berlin, after his first field trip to investigate the ethnobotanical knowledge of the Aguaruna Jívaro, noted that "from a resting spot on a jungle trail, one Aguaruna listed the names of no less than forty distinct trees visible from a fallen tree trunk" and cited reports that a Jesuit priest who resided among the Aguaruna for fifteen years observed that the group recognized at least fifty distinct classes of palms (1970:11). The Huastec Maya recognize and classify 950 species of plants, 70 percent of which have some form of cultural significance (Alcorn and Hernandez 1983). In contrast, from the average contemporary urban dweller one would be fortunate to elicit vernacular names for twenty different kinds of plants. Somewhere in between would lie the average lowland farmer who, depending on age, sex, status, and distance from the market, the irrigation system, or the town center, might have anywhere from fifty to a hundred plant names in his or her everyday vocabulary.

That the contemporary urban dweller survives, one might even say thrives, with his or her woefully impoverished plant vocabulary could argue for the superfluousness of all such extra cultural baggage in this day and age. It may appear that the further one gets from the "primitive" dependence on nature, the more insulated one can afford to be from nature's exigencies and oscillations. Hence, the more one "modernizes," the less one's need for diversity[1] and knowledge thereof, which are only useful for substituting and hedging in a highly uncertain environment. Yet the truth is, modern *Homo sapiens*' dependence has not lessened but has simply shifted: from bare elements of nature to processed ones, from wild progenitors and landraces[2] to domesticated animals and hybrid crops, from "raw" genes to mutant, recombinant, and spliced ones.

In reality, the further one gets from the primitive need for diversity, the greater one's dependency on diversity for short-term productivity and long-term survival. Biodiversity is the ultimate source of nearly all vital raw materials for food, medicine, clothing, shelter, and industry. From diverse flora and fauna come substances for counteracting illnesses, managing fertility, controlling pests, and lubricating machines, as well as genes for breeding in desirable traits, for buffering undesirable side effects of those desirable traits, and for fashioning or "engineering" species to suit human desires and purposes. In the long term, maintaining diversity is the only guarantee of stabilizing the intricate web of life; indeed, it is the key to ecological integrity. Stressing the need to conserve biodiversity, the Keystone Dialogue issued the following statement:

> We, the participants in the Keystone International Dialogue Series on Plant Genetic Resources, choose to speak now in a loud and clear voice, realizing that while the world already has too many crises, it must take heed of yet another. Therefore, we call for a Global Initiative for the Security and Sustainable Use of Plant Genetic Resources. Why? Because we fear that the world's capacity to respond to change is being lost—all too quietly and all too quickly. We can hardly imagine a greater threat to the future well-being of the people of the world than the loss of genetic variability of plants. (1991:2)

Given the inescapable dependence on biodiversity, the question is, How do human beings appreciate, deal with, and protect diverse species or varieties they cannot name or figure out the use for? If cultural recognition and continuous propagation favor maintenance of diversity—a Hanunoo swidden plot, according to Conklin (1954), can have as many as forty different kinds of crops growing simultaneously, while today's monoculture is characterized by one dominant crop—it follows that a cultural repertoire that names, classifies, and utilizes a wider range of variation would be more compatible with ensuring the persistence of that variability. This was emphasized by Victor Toledo when he wrote about diversity with reference to his native Mexico:

> In a country that is characterized by cultural diversity of its rural inhabitants, it is difficult to design a conservation policy without taking into account the cultural dimension; the profound relationship that has existed since time immemorial between nature and culture. . . . Each species of plant, group of animals, type of soil and landscape nearly always has a corresponding linguistic expression, a category of knowledge, a practical use, a religious meaning, a role in

ritual, an individual or collective vitality. To safeguard the natural heritage of the country without safe-guarding the cultures that have given it feeling is to reduce nature to something beyond recognition; static, distant, nearly dead. (Nabhan et al. 1991:127)

CONSERVATION ON TWO FRONTS: GENE BANKING AND MEMORY BANKING

David Clawson (1985) cited several cases of successful maintenance of intra-specific or varietal diversity in traditional tropical agriculture: the Massa of northern Cameroon cultivate five varieties of pearl millet; the Ifugao in the mountain ranges of northern Luzon in the Philippines have at least 200 varieties of sweet potatoes; and farmers in the Andes propagate and exchange thousands of potato clones. Traditional cultures have nurtured diversity, delighting in the mottled appearance of their harvest, in the freedom to choose the kind of rice, wheat, or potato that best fits the occasion or the day-to-day demands of the population. Fowler and Mooney put it this way:

> People used sorghum as a grain, but they also wanted it for making molasses and brooms. There were many species of gourds, valued for such things as food, musical instruments, utensils, and even as penis sheaths. Different types of maize were selected for flour, hominy, popping, boiling, for producing red-colored beverages, and for eating fresh off the cob. Red-kerneled maize was served for ceremonies. When traits people wanted appeared, they were not allowed to be lost but were encouraged, maintained, and perpetuated by the acts of the first farmers. (1990:20)

However, given a production and distribution system that relies on streamlining and simplifying agriculture for greater efficiency and profit as exists in most countries today, one is left with rearguard options for safeguarding plant diversity until such a time that people again come to realize its importance and opt for a drastic change in priorities. One strategy that has been pursued with varying degrees of success by both national and international agricultural research systems is the collection, maintenance, documentation, and evaluation of "representatives" of diversity, that is, samples of various cultivars, landraces, and wild relatives of agricultural crops kept in long-term storage and/or as working collections in gene banks (Plucknett et al. 1987; Holden, Peacock, and Williams 1993). The other strategy, largely neglected and, as I try to demonstrate, a potentially valuable complement, is the parallel collection and documentation of indigenous knowledge and technologies, including uses, preferences, and evaluation criteria associated with traditional varieties of crops—what I refer to as *memory banking*.

International and national research centers have embarked on various programs to collect germplasm of different varieties of staple crops, including rice, wheat, maize, barley, sorghum, millet, potatoes, and sweet potatoes. This is motivated by the recognition that "while breakthroughs in genetic engineering are occurring with increasing speed, options for the future are being foreclosed by the erosion of one of the world's most important heritages, the genetic diversity of our crop plants and their wild relatives" (Plucknett et al. 1987). The germplasm collections can be in the form of cultivated plants, plantlets in tissue culture, or seeds, and are preserved for posterity in well-equipped gene banks that are managed by teams of highly qualified experts (Huaman 1988). The distribution and mandates of the world's gene banks are presented in figure 1.1.

Unfortunately, while genetic accessions[3] are systematically documented, very little cultural information is included in the collection data. The passport data that are routinely collected for each plant accession include such information as varietal name, location and altitude of site, date of collection, and name or institutional affiliation of collector (see sample form for sweet potato in fig. 1.2). It may, but does not always, indicate a local name, and rarely does it contain any data on indigenous technologies, leading one gene bank collector to remark that sometimes the information pertaining to accessions resembles "a skeleton without flesh" (Vaughn 1988, personal communication). Thus one can easily envision a discomforting scenario wherein, when the need arises, the germplasm may still be available in gene banks, but the associated agricultural and postharvest technologies, mostly those traditionally relied upon by local farmers, would no longer be accessible because those who possessed the knowledge have passed away without transmitting what was deemed to be their "archaic" or "obsolete" knowledge.

This indicates a pressing need for the systematic documentation—or memory banking—of indigenous practices of local farmers associated with traditional varieties of staple and supplementary crops. Without this, the genetic information preserved in gene banks will be decontextualized in the sense that the cultural and ecological forces that shaped their selection will be

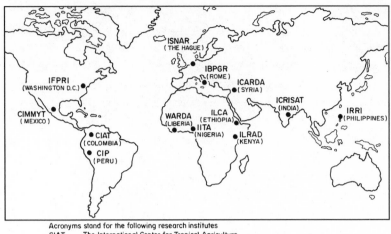

Acronyms stand for the following research institutes
CIAT   The International Center for Tropical Agriculture .
CIMMYT   The International Center for Maize and Wheat Improvement
CIP   The International Potato Center.
IBPGR   The International Board of Plant Genetic Resources.
ICARDA   The International Center for Agricultural Research in the Dry Areas .
ICRISAT   The International Crops Research Institute for the Semi-Arid Tropics.
IFPRI   The International Food Policy Research Institute
IITA   The International Institute of Tropical Agriculture
ILCA   The International Livestock Center for Africa.
ILRAD   The International Laboratory for Research on Animal Diseases .
IRRI   The International Rice Research Institute

Figure 1.1. Distribution and mandates of the world's gene banks. International agricultural research centers within the Consultative Group on International Agricultural Research (from Plucknett et al. 1987).

largely ignored. Given that memories and genes encode information critical to the perpetuation of humanity, I think what is called for is *banking on codes*, or *banking of codes*, for posterity on two fronts: the genetic, on the one hand, which embodies millions of years of biological evolution, and the cultural, which, on the other hand, embodies a long and rough—but often successful—history of human adaptation (fig. 1.3).

   In view of the mutually reinforcing trajectories involving cultural and genetic variability (or, conversely, erosion), certain parallels can be drawn between a gene bank and a memory bank. While germplasm encodes genetic information that has evolved through time as a response to selection pressures, cultural data in the minds of local farmers who have had considerable experience in growing these crops are repositories of coded, time-tested adaptations to the environment. With the present trend in agricultural development, genetic information coded in wild strains and traditional crop varieties or landraces is threatened with erosion as pressure toward more intensive mono-

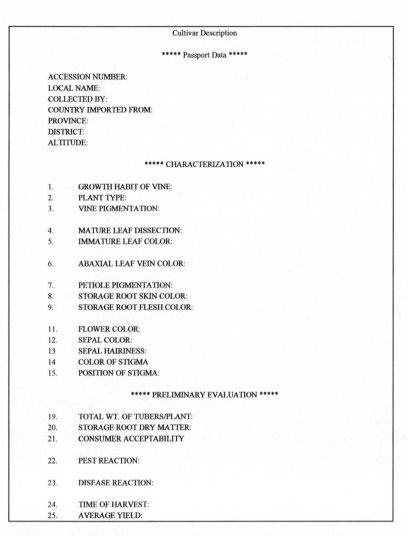

Cultivar Description

***** Passport Data *****

ACCESSION NUMBER:
LOCAL NAME:
COLLECTED BY:
COUNTRY IMPORTED FROM:
PROVINCE:
DISTRICT:
ALTITUDE:

***** CHARACTERIZATION *****

1.   GROWTH HABIT OF VINE:
2.   PLANT TYPE:
3.   VINE PIGMENTATION:

4.   MATURE LEAF DISSECTION:
5.   IMMATURE LEAF COLOR:

6.   ABAXIAL LEAF VEIN COLOR:

7.   PETIOLE PIGMENTATION:
8.   STORAGE ROOT SKIN COLOR:
9.   STORAGE ROOT FLESH COLOR:

11. FLOWER COLOR:
12. SEPAL COLOR:
13   SEPAL HAIRINESS:
14   COLOR OF STIGMA
15. POSITION OF STIGMA:

***** PRELIMINARY EVALUATION *****

19. TOTAL WT. OF TUBERS/PLANT:
20. STORAGE ROOT DRY MATTER:
21. CONSUMER ACCEPTABILITY

22. PEST REACTION:

23. DISEASE REACTION:

24. TIME OF HARVEST:
25. AVERAGE YIELD:

Figure 1.2. Sample passport and evaluation data sheet for sweet potato.

cultural production favors the adoption of newer, higher-yielding cultivars. In a more subtle and pernicious manner, cultural knowledge and practices associated with traditional varieties are in imminent danger of being swamped by modern technologies. Yet, while a lot of attention—both favorable and unfavorable—has been given to the hybrid seed, its coterie of high-input technologies and commercialized market demands and tastes have insidiously slipped by, leading to a situation criticized by Third World scientists and activists as an attack on developing country agriculture through a Trojan horse.

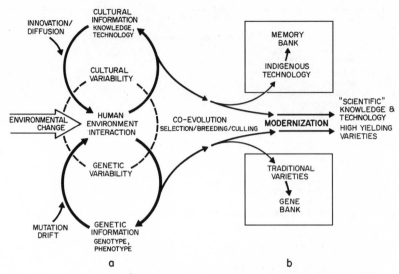

a. Co-evolution of Cultural and Genetic Information Systems. (See also C.J. Bajema, 1972. Transmission of Information about the Environment in the Human Species. Social Biology 19:224-226)

b. Parallelism and Complementation between Gene Bank and Memory Bank.

Figure 1.3. Conceptual framework for memory banking.

The tight interlinkages between culture and biodiversity were recognized in the *Global Biodiversity Strategy* promulgated by the World Resources Institute (WRI), the World Conservation Union (IUCN), and the United Nations Environment Program (UNEP) in consultation with the Food and Agricultural Organization (FAO). According to the *Strategy*, "The loss of genetic, species, and ecosystem diversity both stems from and invites the loss of cultural diversity. Diverse cultures have bred and sustained numerous varieties of crop, livestock, and habitats. By the same token, the loss of certain crops, replacement of traditional crops with export crops, the extinction of species embedded in religion, mythology, or folklore and the degradation or conversion of homelands are cultural as well as biological losses" (1992:11).

A CASE FOR URGENCY

The preservation of genetic variability is imperative, and the concern for this is reflected in the scientific effort to expand and protect the world's germplasm collections. Less recognized but perhaps even more critical is the fact that, with the homogenizing effect of development, variability in terms of technological alternatives and crop choices is becoming narrower and narrower (see fig. 1.3). Largely due to the hegemony of monoculture and capitalism, farmers' options are increasingly restricted to high-yielding varieties and modern agricultural packages proffered by extension agents. Unfortunately, in many developing country situations, this is approaching a point of reification, wherein the existence of alternatives is hardly recognized (Nazarea-Sandoval 1995). Holden et al. emphasized this unfortunate downspiraling trend when they pointed out that

> for all major crops, diversification was at a maximum by the end of the land race phase of crop development. This process is now in reverse. The diversity of land races that supported agriculture for the past 9,000 years is being rapidly eroded and, for some temperate crops, is now nearing completion. This has happened through the substitution of new, genetically uniform cultivars that also have become more uniform through application of increasingly sophisticated agronomic practices, including improved tillage, irrigation, artificial fertilizers, and the chemical control of pests and diseases. . . . The rapid rate of destruction of crop variability is in sad contrast to the rate of its creation—about 100 years compared to 5,000 to 10,000 years. (1993:30)

This problem merits urgent attention. Largely due to the "success" of the Green Revolution, traditional varieties of rice can rarely be found in lowland, irrigated areas of the Philippines at the present time. Because high-yielding varieties of other crops, such as potatoes, corn, and wheat, are presently being developed and diffused in different parts of the world, traditional varieties of these crops may soon suffer the same fate. As a corollary, indigenous technology has been replaced by modern technology at an alarming rate in many areas. As a case in point, many farmers in their fifties and sixties who live in irrigated lowland rice farming areas and came into farming during the Green Revolution's heyday are no longer knowledgeable about traditional methods of rice cultivation. This became evident to me when I was doing my research on agricultural decision making among rice farmers in Kabaritan, Philippines (Nazarea-Sandoval 1995). It is highly probable that within the next decade, as the older generation of farmers, who are now in their seventies or eighties, makes way for the younger generation, much of this valuable cultural information generated and refined by long periods of coevolution will be irretrievably lost. Herein lies the rationale for memory banking: just as the genetic information coded in germplasm can be stored, cultural information in the minds of elderly farmers can be *and urgently needs to be* tapped, documented, and preserved for posterity.

In summary, the motivation behind any germplasm collection is to prevent genetic erosion or, stated more positively, to conserve crop genetic diversity. We should keep in mind, however, that genetic information and cultural information are coevolving systems, and just as farmers from the Agricultural Revolution of the Neolithic onward have developed the landraces that account for the diversity of agricultural crops, one major force in the present decline of biotic diversity worldwide is human intervention. Since the inception of the Green Revolution, selection, breeding, and culling have significantly reduced genetic variation, culminating in the widespread effort to disseminate and promote only the "best" varieties of each food crop. This trend has reached unparalleled proportions in modern times with the premium placed on high yield, short maturity, input sensitivity, and quick turnover for both varieties and technologies. Hence, it would be advantageous if gene banks were complemented by memory banks into which relevant cultural information could be stored for posterity. This could provide a wide range of agricultural scientists and development workers—not to mention rising cohorts of farmers—with insights into sustainable technologies used in the past or potential applications for the future.

FLESHING OUT PASSPORT DATA

This brings us to yet another basic principle behind germplasm collections—that ultimately, their accessions must be usable and useful. According to the 1988 Annual Report of the International Board of Plant Genetic Resources (IBPGR), it "seeks to guarantee the long-term conservation of plant genetic resources, but must also seek to ensure that these materials are used." In reality, much of the material remains underutilized. Observing that only a small fraction of the germplasm collected is actually tapped, Enrique Chujoy, a plant breeder at the International Potato Center, commented that gene banks run the risk of becoming "libraries without readers" (personal communication, 1990). Could this perhaps be due to the fact that the germplasm stores are oftentimes unintelligible to potential users, sterilized as they have been of any background information on why they were cultivated, what they were good (or bad) for, how they were managed, and why they might be useful in the future or in other places? Experience with agricultural development, environmental restoration, soil conservation, and integrated pest management tells us that frequently the most effective solutions to persistent problems could be those that have been applied by indigenous groups for ages rather than those that scientists are expected to concoct in their laboratories (Warren 1984; Lightfoot 1987; Fujisaka 1988; Bentley and Andrew 1991).

An optimistic note in this scenario is that in recent years, the International Board of Plant Genetic Resources (IPGRI, into which IBPGR metamorphosed in 1993) has initiated efforts to integrate what it has termed "socioeconomic and cultural aspects" of plant genetic resources into its genetic diversity program. This new thrust has been institutionalized in a program called Socioeconomic and Cultural Aspects, SECA, directed by a full-time social scientist at IPGRI. This is in response to "a growing concern that indigenous knowledge of cultivated and wild species is being rapidly lost. As societies change, in many cases the younger generations do not acquire the knowledge of their elders" (Toby Hodgkin, quoted in Raymond 1993:19).

In a related development in 1994, the International Rice Research Institute (IRRI) advertised for a full-time social scientist to work specifically with rice germplasm conservation and in 1996 successfully filled this position. This reflected a radical reorientation, considering that IRRI's International Rice Germplasm Center had been staffed mainly with biological and agricultural scientists since its inception. This shift was driven by an increasing realization that "the diversity of the rice crop evolved over thousands of years, as Asian and African peasant farmers—mostly women—selected different types to suit local cultivation practices and needs. This process of selection has led to a multiplicity of varieties adapted to a wide range of agro-ecological conditions, with resistances to insect pests and diseases" (Jackson and Huggan 1991:22).

The value of safeguarding cultural and biological diversity for future generations is clear. In case of drastic and unforeseen changes in the environment, the presence of genetic variability on which natural selection can operate assures that there will be a perpetuation of species and even of life itself. In the same manner, sociocultural evolution works on the cultural variability that exists within any population in terms of knowledge, technology, preferences, and life ways. If this cultural diversity is missing—in this case, knowledge systems coding information about agricultural beliefs and practices—then the population has lost its most significant reservoir of adaptive capability.

In 1990, I proposed memory banking as a parallel and complementary effort to gene banking to safeguard cultural variability along with crop genetic diversity (Nazarea-Sandoval 1990). The objective of the memory banking project was to come up with a thorough documentation of cultural practices associated with traditional crop varieties, starting with sweet potato varieties of the Philippines. A combination of biological and anthropological methods and rural appraisal techniques was used to systematically collect information on technologies and beliefs associated with traditional crop varieties, and to identify key features that formed the basis for local nomenclature, classification, evaluation, and utilization. Participant observation and key informant interviewing were utilized to learn from the farmers of Bukidnon, in the southern Philippines, about their practices and preferences pertaining to choice of planting area, land preparation, procurement and preparation of planting materials, selection of varieties, timing and methods of planting, pest and weed management, maintenance of soil fertility, harvesting, and storage. Then twelve key informants in each area were asked to reconstruct their experiences of growing sweet potatoes from the time of their youth. Their life histories were elicited by informal interviewing, guided whenever necessary by probes to help them reminisce about and describe varieties planted and varieties "lost," appropriate soil types, farming implements used, agricultural calendars and rituals, and methods of preparation and storage.

The key informants were also asked to make diagrams of different varieties of sweet potatoes, including those recalled as well as those in cultivation (but without looking at actual specimens). It was emphasized that it was not really accuracy that was desired as much as their recollection of the characteristics of the different varieties. These cognitive morphological "maps" gave an indication as to what features were most salient in the informants' memories and also give a clue as to the local evaluation criteria for sweet potatoes. Later on, informants were asked to sort and rank the varieties that they were currently cultivating and those they were aware of but were not actually cultivating, giving their own reasons for their particular sorting and ranking schemes. These procedures are discussed in greater detail in the memory banking protocol in chapter 2.

Phase I of the research produced transcripts of taped interviews recording farmers' perspectives about characteristics of, and agricultural practices associated with, traditional sweet potato varieties, as well as their views and recollections of changes that have occurred through their lifetimes with reference to crop diversity and management practices. In addition, we established memory bank files of indigenous technologies, local drawings of different varieties, and local evaluations pertaining to sweet potato landraces and their cultivation in the Philippines (see appendixes A and D). These can serve as a complement to the genetic/agronomic evaluation coded and stored for each variety in the germplasm collection. The implications of the results for the relationships among commercialization, heterogeneity, and marginality are discussed in chapters 3, 4, and 5.

Phase II of the memory banking project consisted of the collaborative establishment of a parcel of land in each region where traditional root crop varieties could be maintained in situ for purposes of retaining and enhancing genetic diversity, verifying local names, and refreshing farmers' (and scientists') memories and serving as a stimulus for taxonomic debates and clarification. Initially, volunteers from each of the ethnic groups in Bukidnon were asked to collaborate with the investigators in planting and caring for a patch of land near the experiment station that could be a repository of traditional varieties of sweet potatoes. The farmers of Bukidnon found the idea intuitively appealing. The local germplasm collection was established in November 1990, in Dalwangan, Malaybalay, and Bukidnon. As a next step, in situ germplasm collections of root crops were initiated nearer to the farmers' fields, with farmers themselves having the greater responsibility in establishment and maintenance. Different forms of curatorship and stewardship over the in situ collections were experimented with, the results of which are discussed in chapter 6.

These efforts were meant to address what has been referred to in a report of a panel of the Board on Science and Technology for International Development, National Research Council, as "the real tragedy of the commons" or the phenomenon wherein "traditional management systems that were effective for thousands of years become obsolete in a few decades, replaced by systems of relentless exploitation of rural people and rural countries, those who depend on primary productivity." Further stressing the urgency of the situation, the report went on:

> Diversity, both biological and cultural, is a casualty of this process and of the operant development paradigm behind it. In the push, for example, to modify local farming systems to accommodate modern Western technologies and to put in place the institutions required to manage these technologies, little heed has been given to the complexity of systems such as tropical rain forests or their indigenous peoples. As more consumptive exploitation of biological resources occurs, cultural diversity is often reduced, for two main reasons. First, a significant portion of cultural diversity that enables people to earn a living from the local biological environment is no longer functional; second, subordinated groups must often imitate the culture of the dominant group, thereby losing a substantial portion of their cultural identity and, hence, their diversity. (National Research Council 1992:92)

The genetic diversity of culturally relevant plants—resources recognized and used by humans for food, medicine, fiber, construction, ornament, and ritual—by no means represents biodiversity in its entirety. However, it is a significant portion that needs urgent attention because it is the most vulnerable to the fast pace of cultural and genetic erosion engendered by modern agriculture, economic development, and political integration. Moreover, "the real tragedy of the commons" will continue to cause irreparable damage to the human legacy of knowledge regarding plant genetic resources unless measures are instituted to protect cultural diversity from mindless homogenization.

2

MEMORY BANKING PROTOCOL

Guidelines toward Systematic Documentation

Scattered works documenting farmers' indigenous practices already exist. With the desired end in view of protecting diversity, what is needed is a way to systematically collect, store, and retrieve information so that potentially useful agricultural knowledge and technologies will continue to be available and accessible. Toward this end, I have developed a methodological framework for supplementing standard procedures for processing gene bank accessions with methods for collecting and storing cultural information. In this chapter, I present and discuss the memory banking protocol to explain in greater detail the nature of the research procedures that we have found useful.

Due to its exploratory nature, the memory banking project in relation to sweet potato cultivation in Bukidnon, Philippines, was a test of methods as much as it was a search for meaningful information. The methods outlined here have proven to be satisfactory and effective in systematically documenting indigenous knowledge and practices associated with traditional varieties of sweet potatoes, and I believe they can be used for collecting information on a wider scale—both geographically and in terms of other important food crops. It may even be possible to integrate some of the methods at the germplasm collection stage so that the passport data can be supplemented, enriched, and contextualized with relevant cultural information. Then, following extensive verification and distillation of information regarding traditional varieties and management practices, those with probable applicability in other areas or in the development of improved cultivars can be passed on to, and utilized by, other farmers, as well as by agronomists, plant breeders, entomologists, plant pathologists, and extension agents, while giving due recognition and, where appropriate, compensation to the sources of the knowledge and the germplasm.

The overall goal of both the memory banking project and the protocol is to help preserve diversity in relation to food crops. Because using is still the best antidote against losing, cultural and genetic diversity are mutually reinforcing both in the upswing (such as during the Agricultural Revolution of the Neolithic) and in the downswing (as in the Green Revolution of more recent vintage). The memory banking protocol is thus designed to complement gene banking procedures in an effort to record and conserve diversity—both biological and cultural—before all is lost. Documentation, reconstruction, and systematization of cultural information pertaining to indigenous knowledge, beliefs, and technologies need to be given more prominence and to be more tightly integrated into gene banking procedures in order for diversity to be given a fighting chance (fig. 2.1).

In retrospect, the first phase of the memory banking initiative was a time for experimentation—not only in terms of data gathering but also in terms of research design. This chapter is a smoothed-out report on the results of our trial and error with our method, or more precisely with a variety of methods. Its more specific, concrete aim is to provide guidelines for researchers from diverse backgrounds—both natural and social, basic and applied science—to document local agricultural knowledge and practices, as well as evaluation criteria and preferences pertaining to traditional varieties of crops. Another version of the protocol has been published to guide local youths in the documentation of their elders' knowledge (Nazarea et al. 1997). This section, in addition, provides the methodological underpinnings for the discussions that follow on commercialization and the distribution of indigenous knowledge, fuzziness and the value of multiple criteria, and cultural experiments in germplasm collection and enrichment.

Because of the complex nature of the subject matter and the fact that for the most part we have to rely on informant accounts, there is a need to pursue an investigation of several dimensions using complementary methods of data collection and analysis. These methods are outlined in the following sections, along with samples of instruments and results. The process of using multiple methods in research as a means of counterchecking and dovetailing information is referred to in the literature as *triangulation* (see, for example,

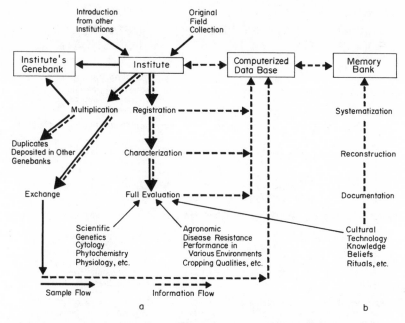

Figure 2.1. Operational framework for integrating memory banking into gene banking: (a) procedures followed in processing a gene-bank accession (from Plucknett et al. 1987); (b) procedures followed in memory banking.

McNabb 1991), and this is the general strategy followed in the memory banking protocol. Thus, for each general procedure proposed for the integration of memory banking data into the full process of the documentation and evaluation of gene bank accessions, three specific methods are presented and their relation to each other discussed. Figure 2.2 illustrates how the various methods are used to triangulate and provide not only a multidimensional perspective on the problem but also a means to compare information from various sources. The domains investigated by the different methods are also specified.

The presentation of procedures in this protocol is processual rather than topical, and it can be used as a step-by-step guide to memory banking. Through an explanation of the rationale, advantages, and pitfalls of each method, the researcher is enabled to use his or her own best judgment on what modifications and adaptations to make to suit the research design to field conditions and other constraints. For example, if the researcher is pressed for time or lacks formal training in the social sciences and feels less than comfortable with some of the ethnographic techniques, he or she can

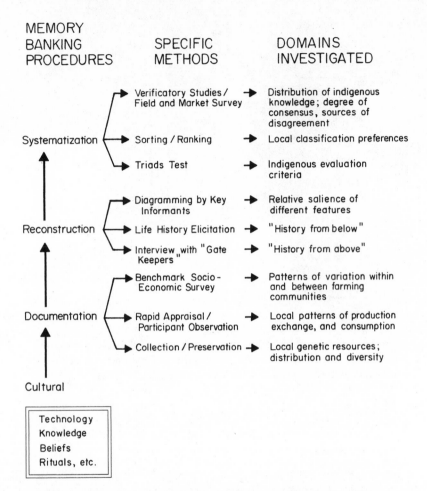

MEMORY
BANKING   SPECIFIC   DOMAINS
PROCEDURES   METHODS   INVESTIGATED

Systematization
- Verificatory Studies / Field and Market Survey → Distribution of indigenous knowledge; degree of consensus, sources of disagreement
- Sorting / Ranking → Local classification preferences
- Triads Test → Indigenous evaluation criteria

Reconstruction
- Diagramming by Key Informants → Relative salience of different features
- Life History Elicitation → "History from below"
- Interview with "Gate Keepers" → "History from above"

Documentation
- Benchmark Socio-Economic Survey → Patterns of variation within and between farming communities
- Rapid Appraisal / Participant Observation → Local patterns of production exchange, and consumption
- Collection / Preservation → Local genetic resources; distribution and diversity

Cultural

Technology
Knowledge
Beliefs
Rituals, etc.

Figure 2.2. Schematic diagram of process and output of memory banking.

choose to leave out one method from each group. (From my point of view, the ones that can be left out with the least amount of damage are the benchmark socioeconomic survey for documentation, the diagramming by key informants for reconstruction, and the triads test for systematization. I must stress that these methods are important in understanding the socioeconomic context, relative cognitive salience of different features, and local systems of classification and discrimination, respectively. However, we can refer to these, in our most conciliatory mood, as "ethnographic luxuries.")

In the final section, the different methods are pulled together and compared with respect to their objectives, respondents, and manageability (table 2.1). Armed with these considerations, the interested researcher can be better informed about decisions in the field that he or she alone can make.

DOCUMENTATION

Collection and Preservation of Specimens

Biological specimens of different varieties are collected and preserved in order to gauge the existing diversity in an area. In addition, because we have to rely on verbal reports and recall data from local informants, it is imperative that there be voucher specimens or "types" to refer to in order to track down and, if possible, resolve sources of inconsistencies. These inconsistencies may emanate either cognitively, from the different backgrounds and statuses of informants (e.g., migration history, ethnic affiliation, occupational history, and gender) or phenotypically, from physical variations in the biological specimens themselves due to differences in growing conditions (e.g., soil, rainfall, temperature, pests, and pathogens). Although the issue of correspondence between local nomenclature and existing varieties cannot be resolved unless biochemical and molecular assays (see, for example, Quiros et al. 1990; Avise 1994) are used for varietal discrimination, the voucher specimens are always helpful as a reference point.

Collection of Specimens

1. Walk around the village and talk with farmers about the crop—what varieties exist, where these can be found, why people cultivate them, and what varieties used to exist in the area but have disappeared and for what reasons. Assume the role of student or apprentice and encourage the local people to point out, identify, and provide samples of varieties being talked about. Some farmers make better informants than others. Be open to opportunities at all times.

2. Secure at least four cuttings of each variety, one for drying and preservation and three for cultivating at the experiment stations. Keep the latter moist in transit.

3. In the case of root crops, whenever possible also obtain three roots per variety. Two will be used for photographing (one whole and one sliced to show flesh color) and one for planting.

TABLE 2.1. Characteristics of Different Methods Used in Memory Banking

Method	Main Objective(s)	Respondent/Informants	Remarks from Experience
Collection/preservation	To provide a physical record or "types" against which local names and evaluations can be checked.	Local farmers can point out and name the different varieties; some are more knowledgeable than others.	Considerable variation in naming varieties, so source of material and information should be carefully documented.
Rapid appraisal/preliminary participant observation	To provide a basis for framing locally relevant questions; also gives some indication as to what directions are worth pursuing.	Willing and accessible informants give the most information within a limited time frame.	Participant observation, even for a limited period, allows one to counter-check reports and paves the way for establishing rapport.
Benchmark socioeconomic survey	To provide hard data which can later be subjected to statistical analysis of central tendencies and trends regarding the community being studied.	Total enumeration would be ideal; where this is not feasible, 20% of the total, randomly selected, would be satisfactory.	Can help one identify bases of internal differentiation and zero in on key informants to represent different groups; quantitative data can be handy when interdisciplinary understanding is sought.
Interview with "gatekeepers"	To get at the "official" version of local events influencing changes in technology and diversity through time.	Local officials, teachers, medicine men, leaders of farmers' and home-makers' associations, rural bank representatives, agricultural technicians, etc.	Indispensable in seeking cooperation for one's project; very useful in providing leads to potential key informants.

Method	Purpose	Informants	Comments
Life history elicitation	To provide a reconstruction of the past through the perspectives of ordinary men and women.	Limited number of key informants, in this case older members of the community who have had considerable experience with the crop.	May ramble unless one is prepared to direct the conversation with timely, tactful, and well-chosen questions; provides a more candid version of developments.
Diagramming from memory	To provide some insight as to the relative importance of different features of the crop for different groups of people.	Limited number of key informants; in this case, older members of the community who have had considerable experience with the crop.	Highly interesting and enjoyed by most informants, but results are subtle and take time to analyze; informants' running commentary help in interpreting diagrams.
Triads test	To provide clues for understanding local perspectives on relationship and contrast among varieties.	Limited number of informants; in this case, older members of the community who have had considerable experience with the crop.	The explanations informants give about their answers are very revealing about local evaluation criteria.
Sorting/ranking	To examine indigenous classification of, as well as preferences for, different varieties; complements triads test in elaborating local perceptions.	Limited number of informants; in this case, older members of the community who have had considerable experience with the crop.	Time consuming but also user-friendly; for nonliterate informants, one can use specimens instead of written names of local varieties.
Verificatory studies/field and market survey	To validate results from limited sample on a broader scale; to fill gaps in information and check inconsistencies.	Broader sample than key informants but more limited than benchmark survey and not necessarily involving the same respondents.	Very useful, but design and execution should be given a lot of thought; otherwise, these methods may further confuse the issues.

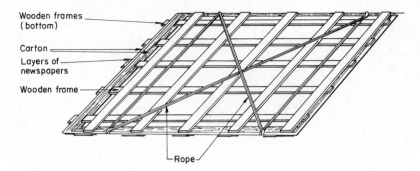

Wooden frames (bottom)

Carton

Layers of newspapers

Wooden frame

Rope

Figure 2.3. Wooden presser for botanical specimens.

Sweet Potato Varieties Of The Philippines

International Potato Center/ User's Perspective

with Agricultural Research and Development

Common name _____ Dialect _____

Collector _____

Locality _____

Province _____

Habitat _____

Altitude _____ meter

Tree, shrub, bush, vine, herb _____

Ht. Of plant _____ m DBH _____ cm

Leaves _____

Flower _____

Fruit _____

Cultural practices _____

Economic Uses _____

Special notes _____

Date _____, 199 __

Figure 2.4. Specimen data sheet used for memory banking.

Preservation of Specimens

1. Treat sweet potato cuttings for preservation as you would most herbarium specimens. After collection, remove any trace of surface soil or moisture, then press specimens between layers of newspapers and bind tightly with wooden frames (fig. 2.3).

2. In the absence of an oven, dry under the hot sun for three to four days, changing newspapers daily to prevent mold growth. If an oven is accessible, oven-dry samples at low temperatures (approximately 150 to 200°F) for one to two days.

3. After drying, mount specimens on thick white herbarium paper such as bristol board. Label carefully, filling in the data sheet as completely as possible (fig. 2.4). At the same time, on separate index cards enter morphological evaluations of the particular variety (Huaman 1988).

Rapid Appraisal and Preliminary Participant Observation

Rapid (actually, not-so-rapid) community appraisal, coupled with preliminary participant observation, is undertaken during the first month of fieldwork to arrive at a working knowledge of the agricultural system and the different "players" or "actors" involved. The former method, of the rapid rural appraisal or RRA genre, achieves the goal of quick information gathering but has been criticized for also being "quick and dirty" in that only the most superficial (and at times incorrect) "roadside" information yields itself to a speedy reconnaissance. The latter method is the stock-in-trade of anthropologists, involving immersion in the community to understand local ways of doing things, of thinking and being. It has, however, been dismissed by some development workers as too cumbersome, inefficient, and "unscientific." Complementing each other, rapid appraisal and preliminary participant observation can familiarize the researcher with local patterns of subsistence and exchange (fig. 2.5), provide him or her with numerous opportunities to establish rapport with the community, and help in framing meaningful questions for the benchmark socioeconomic survey, as well as for subsequent ethnographic procedures.

Places that should be visited—optimal contexts for discussions on varietal composition and varietal choice—include local markets, home gardens, settlements of natives and migrants, traditional fairs and festivities, trading

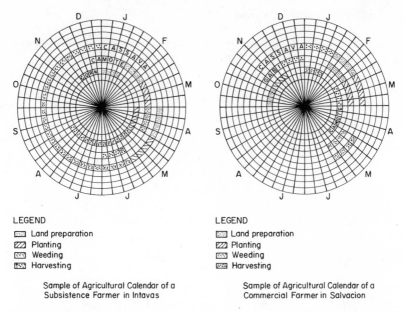

LEGEND

▨ Land preparation
▨ Planting
▨ Weeding
▨ Harvesting

Sample of Agricultural Calendar of a
Subsistence Farmer in Intavas

LEGEND

▨ Land preparation
▨ Planting
▨ Weeding
▨ Harvesting

Sample of Agricultural Calendar of a
Commercial Farmer in Salvacion

Figure 2.5. Sample of agricultural calendars depicting local patterns of subsistence.

stations, and sites of home enterprise or small-scale food processing. To gain the most information from the exchange, investigators should come prepared with a loosely structured (ideally, memorized) interview schedule. Some specific topics that may fruitfully be explored with local informants on such occasions include the following:

1. Information on the population

    a. Are the people mostly natives of the place or have they originated from other places? If from other places, where?

    b. Is the community composed of more young or old, more females or males?

    c. Who are the most knowledgeable or experienced farmers with respect to the crop? Would they be willing to participate in the project?

2. Information on cropping systems

    a. What is the average size of a landholding and what are the major crops planted?

    b. What proportion of the land is devoted to the crop? Has this changed through time? Why?

c. What is the schedule of planting or the agricultural calendar like?

d. What proportion of the produce is for subsistence and what proportion for market? How has this changed through time?

3. Information on diversity

a. Are you or your neighbors still planting traditional varieties? Why or why not?

b. Are you or your neighbors planting more than one variety? Why or why not?

c. Have you tried planting other varieties in the past that you no longer cultivate at present? If so, why? What happened to those varieties?

Benchmark Socioeconomic Survey

This should be attempted only after considerable time has elapsed from one's entry into the community (my personal rule of thumb is only after at least a month of preliminary participant observation). Otherwise, one runs the risk of asking totally out-of-context questions that strain the patience of the respondents and provide no meaningful information on the subject at hand.

A benchmark survey is a more structured way of finding out about the farming system in the area (see appendix B). It also provides valuable insights on the degree and bases of internal differentiation. This is important in deciding how many key informants to choose for the more intensive tasks that follow and what categories (depending on the relevant parameters of internal differentiation) these informants should represent.

1. Depending on one's intent, he or she can use close-ended or open-ended questions or a combination of both. The former type is easier to code during data analysis but is more restrictive in uncovering new insights, whereas the latter type is more challenging to analyze but yields a lot of unexpected, usually significant information.

2. A benchmark survey should be in the local dialect. If translated from English by a native speaker, the translation should be counterchecked by asking another native bilingual speaker to back-translate (i.e., to English). This is done to check whether there are any errors or ambiguities in the translation.

3. It is standard operating procedure to pretest an interview schedule for a benchmark survey on a limited but comparable sample in order to anticipate and correct any vague or problematic questions.

4. Local assistants or enumerators can be hired for administering the survey, but they should first be trained well in the methodology of the survey and overall goals of the research undertaking. Objectives and procedures need to be carefully explained without giving any indication of expected results.

5. There should be only as many interviewers as needed to get the job done. (I prefer two enumerators, even if I have to sample instead of doing a total enumeration when the population is large.) This economy in personnel also forces the researcher to limit the number of questions in order to shorten the interview, thus avoiding the negative effects—particularly informant fatigue—attendant on long and tiring questionnaires. It also minimizes variation in responses that is only an artifact of interviewing style.

RECONSTRUCTION

Interviews with "Gatekeepers"

Interviews with figures of authority in the community, or gatekeepers, can serve as a first step in reconstructing local history, although one should always bear in mind that one is getting only the "official" version. For the purpose of memory banking, this reconstruction should be focused on changes in varieties and technologies through time, factors that brought about these changes, what people thought about these changes, how they were affected personally, and what they would have done differently if they had foreseen the consequences.

Sources of valuable information on local history, specifically that pertaining to agricultural practices and beliefs, include village chieftains or local officials, "best" or most experienced/productive farmers, native healers, and, if they have been in the area for some time, schoolteachers and extension agents. Knowing most of the people in the community, these gatekeepers can also provide leads and introductions and thereby help the researcher identify and secure the collaboration of key informants.

Life History Elicitation

If interviewing gatekeepers enables the researcher to reconstruct "history from above," life history elicitation enables him or her to reconstruct "history from below"; that is, from the experiences of actual cultivators and consumers of the crop. In memory banking, life histories (or oral histories, as the more directed ones are sometimes called) give the investigator a wealth of information on changes in diversity, indigenous knowledge, and practices within the lifetime of several well-chosen informants. The method, however, is interactive, and for this reason a lot depends on the "style" of the interviewer—perhaps more so than any other procedure in this protocol. However, with sufficient sensitivity and respect for other people's dignity, it is possible to establish a partnership between interviewer and interviewee in elucidating events of the past.

1. Outline what kind of information is desired and prepare to work questions around that topic. In our case, the questions revolved around the recollections and perspectives of informants on how varietal composition and agricultural technologies evolved from the time the informant was a child to the time of his or her youth and eventually to the period of maturity and old age. Note that the focus should be on personal experiences and views, not on development in the abstract.

2. Commit the questions or probes to memory; if it will be helpful, design and use codes. For example, one could visualize a matrix of information that is desired from each informant, as presented in figure 2.6.

3. Choose key informants well. Minimally, they should represent gender, ethnic, and socioeconomic variations in the community so that in the end one can construct a well-rounded picture that captures cultural and intracultural diversity. Preferably, key informants should be experienced, intellectually curious, and articulate (which is not the same as having had formal education).

4. Approach the informant and explain the overall goal of the research. I have found that a good way to do this is to say that for years farmers have

	LP	SP	CM	PC	PH
C					
Y					
M					
O					

C = Childhood   O = Old age   CM = Cultural management
Y = Youth   LP = Land preparation   PC = Pest control
M = Maturity   SP = Source of planting materials   PH = Post-harvest

Figure 2.6. Matrix for life history elicitation.

been told what to do, but now we believe it is time to listen and reflect on what they have been doing to survive, given all the constraints. Ask the informant if it is possible for him or her to relate events pertaining to cultivation of the crop that he or she observed—or, better still, participated in—when growing up. Request a block of uninterrupted time—at least thirty minutes, ideally an hour or more—and if it is not feasible at the time the informant is approached, request an appointment to return.

5. Allow the informant to freely and informally narrate his or her story, but be prepared to tactfully direct the conversation back to the topic before it goes too far astray. Record the life histories on tape, but take notes on important points made during the narration. This always helps in the transcription process.

Excerpts of life histories from Bukidnon are presented below. In analyzing life histories it is important to remember that the different versions can be used to complement each other to get a better idea of the evolution of crop diversity and agricultural practices through time. The information can be recorded in the same kind of matrix that was used to elicit the life histories.

My mother was always choosing to plant sweet potatoes when the moon was full and when the clouds were rounded . . . this way we could be sure that the roots would be big and numerous. She also made it a point that the soil was hilled up so the roots would not grow underground.

Sweet potato has served as our only source of food during hard times such as during the dry summer months. We cook the leaves as vegetables and use the roots as "rice." As long as we have sweet potatoes, we will survive.

For fish poisoning or allergies, the sweet potato tops are boiled and the liquid is drunk by the sick person. For skin diseases, the roots are crushed and applied as poultice—the white ones are good for this. If you are poor like us, this kind of treatment is enough.

We plant these varieties now because they are the only ones available, the only ones which were left. If there were other traditional varieties, we would plant them too, for they are more delicious than the new ones.

Some of the old varieties just disappeared because people planted different crops of different varieties. As a result, some of those which were not given any attention slowly vanished.

Diagramming from Memory

Key informants are asked to draw the different varieties of the crop that they can recall. They should be assured that the researcher is not after "accuracy" or faithfulness of rendition but more how informants remember the particular variety. This way, informants will overcome their timidity, and the researcher is assured that those features that are considered more important are given more emphasis in the drawings.

1. As much as possible, try to isolate the informant for this exercise. Otherwise, onlookers will offer unsolicited suggestions and the informant will be distracted.

2. Offer a range of media—colored pencils and pens, crayons, premixed watercolors in small pots, and so on—and invite the informant to use whatever medium he or she feels most comfortable with.

3. Be encouraging, not intimidating, because the informants may not have had any experience with any of the media. Remember always that they do not owe the researcher any drawings. Give them a sheet of paper on which they can first try things out, experiment with their fingers, and so forth.

4. Tape his or her commentary as the drawings are made. These comments are in themselves revealing and will provide useful clues on how to interpret the drawings later.

The analysis of these drawings is based on the premise that in making drawings from mental images people tend to distort proportion and scale—

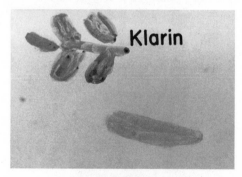

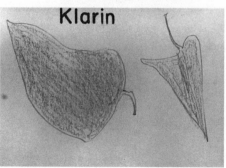

Figure 2.7. Drawings of sweet potato varieties by key informants.

enlarging those features that figure prominently in their daily decisions and minimizing those they consider irrelevant (Berland 1982; Herskovitz 1986). Thus the drawings provide an indication as to what attributes of the different varieties are significant to the local population and which ones are less so. It is also possible to compare different categories of informants (e.g., natives versus migrants, males versus females, commercial growers versus subsistence producers) based on the differences in attention they give to various attributes.

SYSTEMATIZATION

Triads Test

A triads test is an elicitation procedure used in cognitive anthropology to investigate local perceptions of relationship and contrast among items under a domain—in our case, among different varieties of sweet potato. Informants are presented with sets of three stimuli—either cards with names (i.e., of varieties) written on them or actual specimens. The task is for each informant to examine the sets, or triads, and pair two items on the basis of perceived similarity while isolating one on the basis of contrast. Simply put, the informant is asked which item does not belong to the group and why.

1. Assemble a list of all varieties that the people plant or have planted, are consuming or have consumed—in short, those varieties known to many informants. These will constitute the stimuli for the triads test. Written names have the advantage of not influencing through tangible physical attributes the way informants think about the varieties. Actual specimens have the advantage of refreshing memories and also of being useful even for nonliterate informants.

2. Randomize the combinations so that the items have an equal chance of being included in any one triad and there is no particular order by which those expected to be related and isolated (from the point of view of the investigator) are arranged (see appendix C). There is a way to do this by computer using the software Anthropac, by Stephen Borgatti (1996).

3. It is important to give very clear instructions and to stress at the outset that there are no right or wrong answers, that what is being asked for is the informant's perspective on the matter. If, as is often the case, there is a local game that operates on the same general principles, explain the triads test in terms of that game.

4. Each informant should be given ample time to think and ideally should be isolated from others while doing the triads exercise.

The conventional way of analyzing the results of the triads test in cognitive research is to group together items that are frequently lumped together by informants and to try to figure out why the clustering is so. In the form used in the memory banking project, however, the investigator does not stop with the question "Which one does not belong?" but proceeds to ask "Why do you think so?" The reasons given by informants are taken into consideration because these reveal the indigenous criteria for discriminating among varieties. By assessing the relative frequency with which each type of criterion is used, it is possible to infer which ones are most relevant to the local farmers or groups of farmers (see fig. 3.5). It follows (or it should follow) that these are the criteria that plant breeders and agronomists should pay attention to when they engage in agricultural development work.

Sorting and Ranking

Sorting and ranking exercises complement triads tests in eliciting local discrimination criteria. In addition, they give a much clearer indication of local systems of classification and prioritization. Some researchers feel that asking people to sort and/or rank a large array of items may be more intimidating than the triads test, in which they consider only three items at a time. However, I have found that people are more familiar with, and therefore more comfortable with, sorting and ranking tasks because these processes are more akin to mental operations they execute in everyday decision making. By comparison, the triads test is a somewhat more artificial task. Thus, the researcher will have to gauge the informants' predilections and choose or modify as he or she sees fit.

1. In sorting, the informant is presented with an array of items—either names written on cards or actual specimens.

2. The informant is asked to sort the items (or names) into as many piles as he or she wants and to "label" each pile by specifying the categories under which the items are grouped. This can be done by asking why he or she sorted a particular way.

3. The researcher can also request the informant to sort the items into a smaller and smaller number of piles—in other words, to sequentially collapse or combine piles. In this manner, one can see how informants join categories hierarchically, and it is then possible to construct indigenous "taxonomic trees" pertaining to the domain under investigation. It should be kept in mind, however, that such taxonomies are heuristic devices that may at times oversimplify local frameworks.

4. Based on a narrower array of items, the informant is then asked to rank the items by whatever parameter he or she finds meaningful. The informant is later asked to identify what parameter was used.

5. The researcher may subsequently focus on parameters he or she is interested in (e.g., productivity, palatability, resistance, storeability, salability) and ask the informant to sort and rank based on that particular parameter.

Allowing the informant more freedom to decide how many piles to make and what parameters to use as a basis for sorting, ranking, and collapsing enables the researcher to get closer to the indigenous classification system and evaluation criteria, as well as to observe differences among the informants based, for example, on degrees of market integration and gender (see fig. 5.1). In terms of application to agricultural development, this kind of information can give plant breeders, agronomists, and development workers a better understanding of how farmers (and consumers) evaluate the varieties that they are cultivating and consuming or will consider using.

Verificatory Studies (Systematic Field and Market Survey)

Different informants sometimes give different responses to one question or may even give different answers to the same question on different occasions. This, according to our experience, is particularly true for varietal names and attributes. The apparent lack of consensus may reflect either a patterned distribution of indigenous knowledge or simply a disagreement among informants as an artifact of the method of elicitation. One way to rule out the latter is to conduct verification studies to ascertain names and attributes of local varieties.

One method of doing this is by getting samples of varieties (or, in our case, walking the informants through a local germplasm collection) and asking different informants to identify and describe the different varieties. There is presently a lively, ongoing debate about informant consensus, and one of the strongest argued positions is that there is a tendency for convergence toward consensus (Boster 1986; Romney, Weller, and Batchelder 1986). This means that when the majority of informants agree about a particular answer, then the investigator can take that answer to be the culturally correct one with some degree of confidence. An implication of this is that those informants who frequently give answers agreed upon by the majority are the most reliable informants for varietal identification and evaluation. This is of course premised on the fact that names are arrived at by convention and their usefulness is directly proportional to their ability to convey the same idea to different people.

The systematic field and market survey is designed to validate the findings from the more intensive and "softer" ethnographic procedures (e.g., life history elicitation, diagramming, the triads test, and sorting and ranking) on a larger and more representative sample. To conduct this confirmatory survey, informants representing different categories are asked prepared questions (preferably memorized by the interviewer) on aspects about which doubts or gaps exist. In local markets, respondents consist of growers or suppliers, vendors, and buyers. In farmers' fields, male and female farmers (a few in each site) are asked the same set of confirmatory questions. Based on the results of the systematic field and market survey, the information generated by the ethnographic methods—which because of their time-consuming nature can only have a very limited number of key informants—can be verified on a broader scale.

3

MODERNIZATION AND THE DISTRIBUTION OF INDIGENOUS KNOWLEDGE

Development is a powerful and seductive tide that, for better or worse, washes over all sandbags and penetrates to the farthest reaches of the globe. Migration, market integration, and agricultural research and extension all pit local frameworks of understanding and modes of doing against more "modern," "efficient," and "productive" systems of knowledge and technologies. In agriculture, among the most serious casualties of all-out modernization and commercialization are confidence and pride in local farming practices, and the intergenerational transfer of age-old wisdom pertaining to the sustainable use of resources. Along with this comes a negative impact on the nurturance of a variety of traditional crops for their very specific roles in the cultural and social lives of the people. In *Conserving Biodiversity: A Research Agenda for Development Agencies*, the National Research Council called attention to the fact that

> the cultures that developed and maintained local knowledge, and the systems that sustained productivity and diversity over many generations, are rapidly changing. Local knowledge is being replaced by technologies that have not demonstrated their sustainability or long-term contribution to society. As development agencies seek to understand the traditional forms of management, research must seek to identify the nature of this productivity and sustainability from the perspective of the cultures in which they evolved, and it must do so before this knowledge is lost. (1992:105–106)

There are two important considerations to be kept in mind pertaining to the relationship between intensiveness of agriculture and loss of biodiversity. The first is that the trend toward commercialization has precariously whittled down the genetic and cultural base of local farming populations. Hawkes pointed this out in connection with "miracle" or high-yielding varieties:

> The new varieties created by breeders, such as the green revolution 'miracle' wheats and rices, or varieties bred from them, have in fact been so successful that in very many countries they have replaced the extremely variable landraces. Better farming practices have also eliminated the weedy races around the field borders that occasionally exchanged genes with the crops through hybridization and hence increased their diversity. Extension workers and agricultural advisory officers are also constantly advising farmers not to grow the highly diverse mixtures of landraces that were part of their traditional heritage but to select one sort only, or to use selected seed provided by the government, thus discarding the remaining. (1991:6–7)

However, the second, equally important consideration is that the hegemony is never complete. The much-praised and much-maligned Green Revolution of the 1960s and 1970s, for example, primarily affected farmers in lowland, for the most part irrigated, areas of the developing world. In more marginal environments, where new technology and inputs were not readily available, farmers still retained their traditional technologies and varieties (Dempsey 1992). Being predominantly subsistence-oriented, farmers in these marginal areas were also relatively insulated from market demands and price fluctuations. Stephen Brush (1990, 1992) demonstrated that marginal farmers retained varieties of potatoes despite the adoption of "improved" varieties— products of agricultural research and extension—and suggested that diversity rebuilds over time as long as farmers' choices play a role in crop selection.

In this chapter and the next, we will examine local farmers' criteria and decision-making frameworks pertaining to varietal and technology choice. The effects of commercialization will be investigated by analyzing the differences in evaluation criteria between farmers involved in subsistence production versus those engaged in a semicommercial mode of production. Then, as a further step in following the trajectory of modernization, scientists' evaluations of local technologies pertaining to sweet potato production and postharvest handling will be examined in order to tease out some points of convergence and divergence between farmers' perspectives and those of Western science.

A DIFFERENCE OF DEGREE: PRODUCTION FOR SUBSISTENCE AND FOR SALE

The memory banking project focused on two sites. One was Sitio[1] Intavas, in the municipality of Impasug-ong, an upland area on the slope of Mt. Kitanglad (1,200 meters above sea level); the other was Sitio Salvacion, in the municipality of Libona, on a plateau 303 meters above sea level, near the expansive pineapple plantation of the multinational agribusiness corporation Del Monte. Both sites are located in the province of Bukidnon, on the island of Mindanao, where waves of migrants from Luzon and Visayas have interacted, traded, and intermarried with the local population—superimposing and reworking agricultural technologies to fit existing environmental and socio-economic conditions (fig. 3.1).

Writing about global trade and local transformations in Philippine social history, Ronald Edgerton described Bukidnon society at the turn of the nineteenth century as

> characterized by swidden farmers cultivating widely separated up-
> land regions, some of which had supralocal leaders, and residing
> in scattered settlements of interrelated families presided over by
> *tulugan* chiefs and a number of lesser *datus*. In the last decades of
> the century, these people were drawn more and more tightly into
> the web of northcoast culture by traders anxious to barter for their
> produce; by Augustinian, Recollect and Jesuit priests concerned for
> their souls; and by the Spanish government determined to halt the
> spread of Islam in Mindanao. Together, these outside forces affected
> change in Bukidnon economic life and in settlement patterns, and
> they speeded up the process of acculturation as well. (1981:365–366)

The older residents of Intavas, now in their eighties and nineties, remember the Intavas of their youth as being a thickly forested area inhabited by native Bukidnons. Tall trees grew so densely in some parts that "a *carabao*[2] would

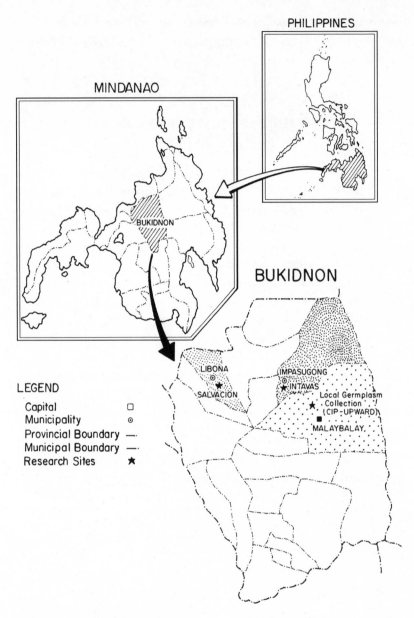

Figure 3.1. Location of study areas.

not be able to pass through." There were some clearings created through slash-and-burn where the natives planted root crops (referred to as *lagutmon*, or famine food), bananas, and coffee. The Bukidnons also gathered bamboo for house construction, split abaca (a fibrous relative of the banana) for bartering with lowlanders, and subsisted on wild beans. The Bukidnons had different tribal affiliations and frequently engaged in intertribal warfare among themselves and against the Muslims inhabiting the same general area. There are, in fact, two versions from oral histories of where the name of the sitio originated, both of them related to internecine warfare but also giving an interesting indication of the state of the vegetation and centrality of plants to human affairs in those days. According to one version, boundaries between tribes were delineated either by thick growths of plants such as cogon, bamboo, rattan, and certain trees, or by geographical features such as streams and hills. If one crossed these boundaries, he was liable to get his head chopped off, or *tabas*. A second version is that when peace was made between previously warring factions, they would chop down, or *tabas*, the vegetative barriers separating them.

By the 1950s, the area was still sparsely populated. There were no roads and no means of transportation, but around this period the first outsiders started trickling in. First came the Boholanos to sell clothes to the natives, accepting, in exchange, abaca, corn, and sugarcane that the latter had started cultivating on a larger scale. Then came the Dumagats (migrants from "across the seas," or the Visayan islands of Cebu, Leyte, Bohol, and Negros). They plowed the land and planted corn along with the taro, yam, and *lutya* (a relative of taro with significantly bigger roots and leaves).

In the 1960s and 1970s, migrants from Luzon, particularly Igorots from the Mountain Province, came to Intavas in search of fertile land, high elevation, and a cool climate for cultivating semitemperate vegetables such as cabbage, potato, pepper, carrot, and tomato. They found growing conditions in their former home almost exactly replicated in Intavas, the only difference being the greater availability of land in the frontier territory. Some Bukidnons and Dumagats, noting the success of the new migrants, tried their hand at growing vegetables, but they had no experience, at best wavering patience, and little capital. Traditional crops like corn, coffee, and banana needed no fertilizer and very little pest and weed management, while Igorot "gardens" needed large doses of all three in order to bring a profit. To this day, many native Bukidnons still insist that they will "go hungry" if they shift to cultivating vegetables for the market.

There was considerable intermarriage between Bukidnons, Dumagats, and Igorots, and agricultural technologies and crops unevenly diffused in different directions over time. Agriculture was—and is—the main source of subsistence and income. Credit was available from financiers, many of them businessmen of Chinese origin, from the nearby city of Cayayan de Oro. The financiers provided capital for all inputs. Then one of two arrangements prevailed at harvest time: in the first, the financier would set a price for the entire product, deduct all the expenses for inputs, and split the remainder, with 40 percent going to the financier and 60 percent going to the farmer who provided land and labor. The alternative arrangement was for the financier to collect all the produce at harvest time and from the sale deduct expenses plus 10 percent interest on credit extended for inputs. The difference would go to the farmer.

Around the 1980s, many of the original Igorot migrants left Intavas and moved on, due, according to our informants, to declining soil fertility. The ones who stayed were those who had intermarried with the natives. Some Dumagats and a few Bukidnons are still planting vegetables using intensive "gardening" technologies introduced by the Igorots, but most continue to engage in subsistence production of root crops. Of the former, many are being financed by urban-based financiers in their commercial ventures, but there are plans to set up a cooperative supported by the Land Bank for the procurement of inputs. This is expected to reduce the dependence of agricultural producers on financiers.

Like Intavas, Salvacion, our second site, was also originally populated by native Bukidnons. Then, between 1940 and 1950, there was an influx of Dumagats from the Visayan islands of Cebu, Bohol, Leyte, and Negros into the area. The Dumagats, joined by migrants from other parts of Mindanao, cleared the largely uncultivated land. According to early settlers, they felled huge trees and also cleared areas overgrown with *cogon*. In the process, most of the natives were driven to more remote, elevated areas like Sil-ipon and Putihon. Hence, there are very few native Bukidnons remaining in the area. The name Salvacion comes from "salvation," because the sitio served as a refuge for migrants from all over Mindanao and the Visayan Islands during the Japanese occupation.

The older generation of Salvacion farmers recall that the area was still in "the wild state" in the early 1950s and into the 1960s. Then people started putting more and more land to cultivation. They planted corn—their staple food in the Visayan Islands where they originated—along with taro, lutya, sweet potato, and cassava. Later, they also planted coffee. But people continuously moved about during this period within the province of Bukidnon and the entire island of Mindanao. Nothing was considered permanent, and very few people owned land. Still, more migrants arrived, particularly those with relatives in Salvacion who were attracted by success stories to try their luck in the new territory.

Not all stories had happy endings, however, for the very fertility of the plateau and the industriousness of its people attracted outside entrepreneurs to take advantage of the situation. As Fay Cooper Cole reported:

> Ultimately, a surplus of coffee, hemp, and cacao led to increased trade with the Visayan city of Cagayan on the coast, and for a time it appeared that the efforts of the Jesuits were resulting in the establishment of a self-supporting community. Unfortunately, these friendly, helpful efforts were not shared by certain well-to-do caciques of the coast or by the Chinese merchants. Parties of Bukidnon, laden with produce, would go to Cagayan, where their innocence of trade and finance was taken advantage of. Low prices for their products were paid in trade for overvalued objects they desired. Many were induced to go into debt and signed papers that led to virtual peonage. When they did not appear as scheduled with hemp and other products, the lenders would secure a judgment and then would go inland to collect. (1956:14)

Still, through *bayanihan* (community self-help) effort, a public school, a small chapel, and a town plaza were constructed in the sitio in the 1970s. Increasingly, land became titled and migrants who decided to leave would sell their land to new migrants. Therefore, as private ownership of land increased, later waves of migrants no longer had easy access to land. Fanning out, landless farmers utilized public lands, fragile hilly lands, and marginal areas. Although tenancy and sharing arrangements were common, landowners became more and more vigilant, preventing squatting on their property.

There were two other developments in the early 1980s that signalled greater stratification and commercialization in Salvacion. As the Del Monte Corporation expanded its pineapple plantations, many landed farmers found it lucrative to rent out portions of their landholding to the giant multinational agribusiness enterprise. Thus there was even less land available for tenancy arrangements, thereby transforming many of the agrarian relationships to that of wage labor. Also at around this time, financiers from the city entered the area and offered capital for inputs in exchange for control over produce. Production of vegetables, coffee, and sweet potato became increasingly commercialized.

Not surprisingly, there was considerable agrarian unrest from the 1970s into the 1980s. Disgruntled over the scarcity of land and the less than equitable labor and credit arrangements, many migrants returned to their places of origin, but others joined the radical New People's Army (NPA), claiming that they were being neglected and marginalized by the government. By the late 1980s, however, NPA supporters were asked to surrender and were offered considerable government support and incentives. Gradually, peace returned to Salvacion, and agricultural production intensified. Although land distribution is still very uneven—ranging from zero to forty hectares per household—there was a resolution in 1992 to give each landless family at least one hectare of land to farm.

Presently, the people of Intavas—composed of native Bukidnons, migrants from Visayas collectively known as Dumagats, and migrants from the Mountain Province of Luzon collectively referred to as Igorots—cultivate different varieties of sweet potatoes side by side and harvest what they like on a staggered basis. People regard sweet potatoes as *tambal sa gutom*, or a "cure for hunger." As one farmer put it, "Even during the dry season, a sure harbinger of hard times, sweet potato does not die and will always produce edible roots. If we have nothing to eat, we just harvest this crop—roots as well as leaves—and our hunger problem will be solved." Because of this, farmers in Intavas view the sweet potato as a subsistence crop, selling only what cannot be consumed by the family and their pigs. Commercial crop production is concentrated on semitemperate vegetables such as cabbage, sweet pepper, and tomato—agricultural options that were introduced by the migrants from the Mountain Province. Other important cash crops in Intavas include corn, coffee, and, to a lesser extent, cassava.

Nevertheless, many people in Salvacion, mostly Visayan migrants, cultivate sweet potatoes on a moderate commercial scale. Note that in Salvacion there was never any significant Igorot migration, so commercial vegetable gardening was never a highly visible agricultural option. Also, by way of comparison, Salvacion is less remote than Intavas, markets are more accessible, and thus the incentive to commercialize is stronger. Some farmers have found sweet potato production to be more lucrative than corn production. Consequently, in terms of land use, an increasing proportion of space is being converted to fields for sweet potato production. One farmer who grows and mar-

TABLE 3.1. Degree of Commercialization of Sweet Potato Production in Study Areas

Percentage of Sweet Potato–Growing Households	Study Area	
	Intavas	Salvacion
Eating and giving away 100% of total production	70.6	54.4
Selling less than 30% of total production	19.6	19.3
Selling between 30% and 60% of total production	9.8	21.0
Selling over 60% of total production	0	5.3

kets sweet potatoes calculated its profitability this way: "As I compared the two crops, one plant of corn can bear two ears, while one cutting of sweet potato can produce six roots. If you try to sell them, sweet potato tubers will earn ₱60.00 per can while corn will earn ₱25.00 per can.[3] In addition to that, you can harvest three times a year with sweet potatoes on a staggered basis, while with corn you can only harvest once a year."

In short, the agricultural system in Salvacion is currently more commercialized than that in Intavas, primarily as a result of its geographic location and its ethnic composition. But it must be emphasized that the difference between Intavas and Salvacion in terms of commercialization of sweet potato production is a matter of degree (table 3.1). While there is a significant trend toward commercialization in Salvacion, more than half of the sitio's farmers are still engaged in production for subsistence. Twenty-one percent of the farmers in Salvacion sell 30–60 percent of their produce, compared to Intavas' 9.8 percent who sell that much. Only 5.3 percent of Salvacion farmers sell over 60 percent of their produce, compared to none who sell that much in Intavas. Comparing the two sites therefore provides us with insights on the concomitants of commercialization of crop production, with the advantage of seeing subtler differences in a state of transition before a state of polarity is reached. With respect to crop diversity at the interspecific level, we can see from figure 3.2 that overall diversity—here indicated indirectly by the number of people planting each crop—is greater in Intavas than in Salvacion. This is so on two central parameters of diversity, that is, the greater number of kinds of crops planted and the greater uniformity or evenness of frequency of different crops.

More specifically, an initial reconnaissance and benchmark survey of the two areas showed less diversity in Salvacion than in Intavas in terms of both the actual number of sweet potato varieties cultivated and the number of varieties known but not actually cultivated (table 3.2). The former can be

Farmland

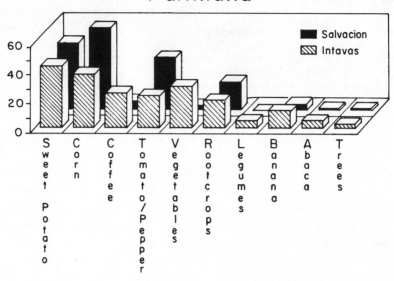

Home Garden

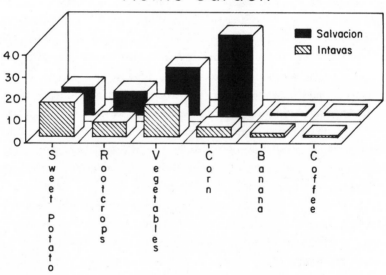

Figure 3.2. Crops planted by farmers in their farmlands and home gardens.

TABLE 3.2. Genetic Diversity of Sweet Potatoes in Intavas
and Salvacion

Intavas		Salvacion	
Varieties Cultivated	Varieties Known but Not Cultivated	Varieties Cultivated	Varieties Known but Not Cultivated
lambayong	linggatos	kasindol	70-days
Valencia	mamugyang	klarin	initlog
lamputi	baliti	katimpa	katumpi
5-finger	kabusot	tapol	sinador
si-uron	saisyenta	dalisan	binangkal
Imelda	dumokot	5-finger	
camba	Sil-ipon	Igorot	
initlog	dalian	kabato	
Malaybalay	hayang-dading	Valencia	
kalugti	granula	katibor	
kabusok	laguitas	kinampay	
Kalibu	kabusog	tinangkong	
Hinapon	Zamboanga	kamada	
ubihon	palapag	buwan-buwan	
tinangkong	inaglar	Arabia	
Manobo	dumakot	kaboholk	
kalibre	gilang	Amerikano	
tulay	kinsuon	languitlit	
Arabia	kayagas	Imelda	
kulating	inapog	Sil-ipon	
gireng-gireng	klarin	kaligatos	
kauyag	guti	katapok	
sugahak	kampol	agorol	
binawin	kalatig		
sabat	Siñorita		
lawaton	kayapas		
dinagat			
amerikano			
siquihor			

Note: The varietal names that start with capital letters indicate places of origin or names of people in whose honor the variety is named.

attributed to the greater degree of commercialization of sweet potato production in Salvacion as a consequence of a stronger pressure to conform to more uniform market demands. Yet the more marked disparity between the number of varieties known in the two sites indicates that knowledge is the first to go, even before genetic erosion sets in. We can see, for example, that the difference between the two sites in terms of the actual number of varieties planted is six, while the difference in terms of varieties known though not cultivated is twenty. This clearly signifies that there is a narrower discrepancy in terms of actual crop diversity than in terms of cognized crop diversity. The results, indicating a faster rate of attrition of agricultural knowledge (more specifically, cognition of diversity) than of genetic diversity itself, underline the need to document indigenous knowledge and technologies before these are swamped by the homogenizing effect of agricultural and economic development.

INDIGENOUS DECISION-MAKING CRITERIA

Human selection is regarded as a pivotal force in defining the fate of landraces, yet both the criteria and the process remain largely a mystery (Hodgkin and Ramanatha Rao 1992). Farmers' evaluation criteria as they consider their options regarding technologies and varieties are of critical significance in understanding cultural and genetic diversity, as well as erosion. What features do farmers pay attention to as they decide which varieties to keep and which to boot out—either deliberately or through neglect? Is there a difference between different kinds of farmers—for example, between commercial farmers and more subsistence-oriented ones, or between males and females—in the kinds of distinguishing features that are more salient and thus more weighty in their decision making? Because humans play a dominant role in the persistence or disappearance of many species of plants, particularly food crops, it follows that the more one finds out about the "calculus" employed, the closer one gets to explaining trends in genetic erosion and to being able to do something to counter them.

In an attempt to further dissect the local bases for varietal discrimination and classification, two triads tests were designed. Although there was some overlap, there were different sets of sweet potato varieties grown and known in Intavas and Salvacion; hence, two different triads tests of randomly generated combinations were constructed (see appendix C). Twelve key informants in each community performed the triads test. As explained in the methods section, the task was for each of the informants to examine each set of three and pair two stimuli (in this case, varieties) on the basis of perceived similarity while isolating one on the basis of perceived contrast. For example, an informant might say varieties 1 and 3 are both sweet, while variety 2 is bland; another informant might say varieties 1 and 2 are both dry, while variety 3 is wet. After this test was accomplished, it was possible to categorize the criteria used by farmers in discriminating among the different varieties.

The results of the triads tests are graphically presented in figures 3.3 and 3.4. The left column designates the informants, while the test item numbers on the top code the triad combination used as stimulus (these can be referred to in appendix C). The shading of the corresponding squares indicates the criteria used by the informant in grouping/differentiating the three varieties comprising each test item. When the squares are left unshaded or blank, it means that the informant gave no response for that particular test item, most of the time because he or she was not familiar with the variety used as a stimulus. When the squares are divided by a diagonal slash, this means that two kinds of criteria were employed by the informant.

From a close examination of the responses to the triads tests, it was discovered that the local criteria that are commonly used in discriminating among sweet potato varieties are

1. morphological—basic structure or appearance without any reference to cultivation requirements, e.g., rounded or elongated, big or small;

2. gastronomic—evaluation of palatability or desirability of the variety as food, e.g., sweet or bland, wet or powdery;

3. life habits—physiological and ecological adaptations of the variety, e.g., produces many or few roots, initiates roots at the bottom only or also at the vine internodes;

4. familiarity—an indication of whether the variety is newly introduced or has been there for some time, whether it is well known or relatively obscure;

5. functional—use value attached by the local population to the particular plant, e.g., whether it is primarily the roots or the leaves that are utilized as food.

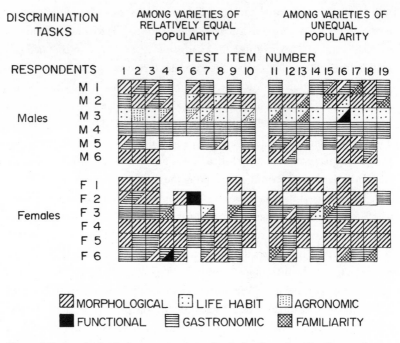

Figure 3.3. Local criteria for sweet potato discrimination, classification, and evaluation in Intavas.

The criteria used by the local farmers and the frequency with which each was used are detailed in table 3.3. The criteria are listed according to relative importance, that is, from the most frequently used to the least frequently cited. Subtotals by criteria and by informant category are also given to facilitate comparison. By way of summary, the relative importance of the local criteria for varietal evaluation is presented as a histogram in figure 3.5.

One significant finding from the triads test results is that morphological and gastronomic criteria are the most frequently employed by the local farmers in discriminating among different varieties. By comparison, agronomic and functional criteria, believed by many agricultural scientists to be the most important, are the least frequently used. Researchers who have studied other crop systems have come up with slightly different orderings of local priorities. Van Oosterhout (1993) reported that the criteria used by African farmers in classifying and selecting sorghum varieties center around gastronomic, maturity, and agronomic considerations. He further asserted that "morphologi-

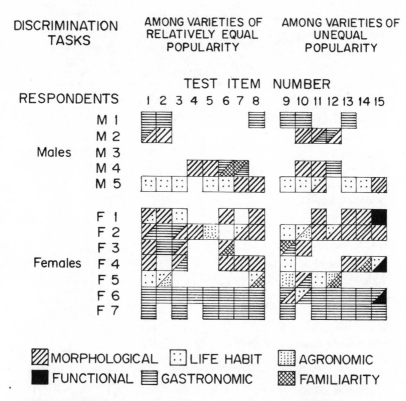

| DISCRIMINATION TASKS | AMONG VARIETIES OF RELATIVELY EQUAL POPULARITY | AMONG VARIETIES OF UNEQUAL POPULARITY |

TEST ITEM NUMBER

RESPONDENTS 1 2 3 4 5 6 7 8   9 10 11 12 13 14 15

Males   M 1
         M 2
         M 3
         M 4
         M 5

Females F 1
         F 2
         F 3
         F 4
         F 5
         F 6
         F 7

▨ MORPHOLOGICAL ⬚ LIFE HABIT ▦ AGRONOMIC
■ FUNCTIONAL ▤ GASTRONOMIC ▩ FAMILIARITY

Figure 3.4. Local criteria for sweet potato discrimination, classification, and evaluation in Salvacion.

cal criteria which have received the bulk of plant breeders' attention are of little importance to farmers" (89). Farmer selection relative to local varieties of soybean, maize, cassava, and sweet potato in the Indonesian islands of Lomboc and Sumbawa revolves around a complex interaction of factors—agronomic, consumer preference, and socioeconomic conditions— embedded in the food system (van Dorp and Rulkens 1993). These results, while differing in some details, all point to the need to pay greater attention to farmer preferences, such as visual appeal and palatability, in addition to the more frequently utilized agronomic characteristics, like yield and hardiness, in evaluating, breeding, and promoting cultivars. To a certain extent the results may also explain why well-meaning (and well-funded) efforts to promote some high-yielding varieties do not always succeed. Lastly, the triads test results indicate the need to keep in mind that farmers are consumers,

TABLE 3.3. **Frequency of Use of Evaluation Criteria by Informant Category**

Criteria	Intavas Female	Intavas Male	Salvacion Female	Salvacion Male	Subtotal by Criterion
A. Morphological					
1) color of skin	16	32	11	3	62
2) color of flesh	34	8	9	7	58
3) size of roots	8	19	7	5	39
4) shape of roots	12	8	7	1	28
5) shape of leaves	2	2	2	3	9
6) color of leaves	2	0	2	2	6
7) size of leaves	1	0	1	1	3
8) texture of skin	1	0	0	0	1
Subtotal by informant category	76	69	39	22	206
B. Gastronomic					
1) texture of flesh	32	16	32	3	83
2) taste of flesh	11	14	37	3	65
3) side effects, e.g., colic	1	0	0	0	1
Subtotal by informant category	44	30	69	6	149
C. Life habits					
1) prolificness of root production	1	12	11	4	28
2) points at which roots are produced	0	2	3	8	13
3) length of maturation period (of roots)	0	0	5	1	6
4) prolificness of leaf production	0	1	0	0	1
Subtotal by informant category	1	15	19	13	48
D. Familiarity					
1) well-known vs. not well-known	4	1	0	2	7
2) traditional vs. new variety	0	1	1	1	3
Subtotal by informant category	4	2	1	3	10
E. Agronomic					
1) hardiness of crop	0	5	1	0	6
2) ideal period of planting	1	1	0	0	2
3) resistance to pests	0	1	0	0	1
Subtotal by informant category	1	7	1	0	9
F. Functional					
1) value of leaves as food	2	0	4	0	6
2) value of roots as food	1	0	1	0	2
Subtotal by informant category	3	0	5	0	8
Total	129	123	134	44	430

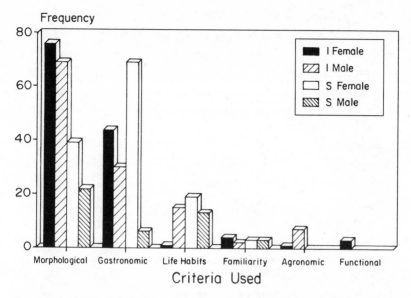

Figure 3.5. Relative importance of local criteria for sweet potato varietal evaluation (based on triads test results). The bars indicate males and females in Intavas and Salvacion.

too, not just producers, and that a significant degree of subsistence orientation is retained in many farming communities.

Dissecting further, the most frequently cited morphological criterion is skin color, closely followed by flesh color. Root size and root shape are also salient, while leaf attributes are given less attention. In terms of gastronomic criteria, flesh texture appears to be more important than flesh taste. This is borne out by the observation that having watery, soft flesh is locally more condemning for sweet potato varieties than having bland taste, a feature that makes the latter good substitutes for rice during lean times. The presence of undesirable side effects such as colic and flatulence is given minor notice. Observations on life habits center on prolificness of root production, followed by a related consideration, the points at which roots are initiated, that is, whether roots are initiated only at the end or also at leaf internodes. Period of root maturation, which would have an important implication on rate of turnover, is not given as much attention as would have been expected, and even fewer comments have to do with leaf production. In terms of familiarity, local farmers comment more frequently on whether a variety (or varieties) is well known or obscure than on whether it has been with them for a long time or not. Agronomic considerations focus on hardiness of the crop, but timing or ideal period of planting and resistance to pests are also considered. Finally, with respect to functional criteria, the value of leaves as food is used more frequently in discriminating among varieties than the value of roots as food. This is due to the fact that while the roots of most varieties are consumed, certain varieties are preferred for the quality of their leaves as vegetables and as medicine.

In terms of distribution of indigenous knowledge or, more specifically, patterning of evaluation criteria with respect to degree of commercialization and gender of informant (see table 3.3 and fig. 3.5), morphological features are more important than gastronomic criteria for the more subsistence-oriented farmers of Intavas. This may appear to be counterintuitive, but it can be explained by the fact that subsistence farmers pay a lot of attention to morphological features divorced from agronomic or market considerations, frequently praising some varieties as *guapo kaayo*, or extremely handsome. Gastronomic criteria (which have a direct bearing on salability) are more important to the commercial producers of Salvacion. Familiarity and agronomic considerations are likewise more prominent for the farmers of Intavas, while life habits (which influence productivity) and functional value (which determines marketability) are more important to the farmers of Salvacion. In terms of gender differentiation, a greater number of criteria are utilized by female farmers compared to male farmers in both communities, perhaps indicating a more detailed observation of—and greater familiarity with—the crop. Moreover, there appears to be a greater differentiation in the number and type of criteria employed by males vis-à-vis females as commercialization of production progresses. This is consistent with the increasing specialization of productive activities between males and females concomitant with market integration.

It should be noted, however, that practically all criteria have economic undertones. Color of flesh, texture of flesh, prolificness of root production, familiarity, hardiness, and value as food, for example, all have implications— and these were alluded to by the informants themselves—for the desirability, marketability, and profitability of the different varieties. It is for this reason that no purely "economic" category was deemed necessary in categorizing the different criteria. Along the same vein, the earlier argument I made about keeping in mind that farmers are consumers too can be extended somewhat to take account of farmers' sensitivity to the demands of other consumers like themselves in their choice of varieties.

A DIFFERENCE IN SCRIPT: SCIENTISTS AND FARMERS ON INDIGENOUS TECHNOLOGIES

Moving a little further along the gradient of modernization, it is instructive to juxtapose local agricultural knowledge and practices with scientists' perspectives on these same practices. The goal is to identify points of convergence and divergence between farmer scripts and scientist scripts in relation to technologies and crops, and the possible bearing these may have on agricultural research and development. Comparing indigenous knowledge with scientific knowledge allows us to follow the trajectory from context-specific, experiential, and culturally appropriate frames of understanding and plans of action to more universalized but nonetheless Western-based ways of knowing and prioritizing.

As used here, a *script* is a program or protocol for orchestrating how things are done and how they are communicated. Farming, after all, is a performance in much the same way that science is a performance (Richards 1985).[4] Both performances require a script. A script is a little more complex than a set of evaluation criteria because it incorporates not only the elements but also the process and the synergy that the process generates. For science, the script is centered on the scientific method—a systematic, rigorous methodology of proof and disproof that is well understood by its disciples. In farming, the script is based on the farmers' own understanding of what they consider to be significant factors and relationships in their environment, and how these can be combined into a workable whole.

Literature on agricultural decision making strongly points to the internal coherence and adaptive significance of indigenous technologies (Rhoades and Booth 1982; Chacon and Gliessman 1982; Nazarea-Sandoval 1991). A closer examination provides interesting evidence that in dealing with similar problems and working toward nearly identical goals—greater productivity and sustainability of agriculture—farmers and scientists nonetheless utilize different criteria and scripts for evaluating options, managing resources, and formulating strategies. The difference can be illustrated in simple terms—for example, by the tendency of rice scientists to focus on "how rice grows," whereas rice farmers are more interested in "how to grow rice" (Rhoades and Bebbington 1995). This is roughly equivalent to Lévi-Strauss's (1966) distinction between "science of the abstract" and "science of the concrete," respectively. From these parallel frameworks, the output of scientists may be seen to consist of findings expressed in neat tables and graphs in research publications. By contrast, the output of the farmers may be viewed as consisting of food, energy, and, ultimately, survival.

Clearly there is a difference in orientation and motivation, not to mention constraints, between farmers and scientists. But while the above dichotomies are fundamentally true, they dramatize just a little bit more than they illuminate—as dichotomies are wont to do. Column 1 in table 3.4 presents a list of indigenous beliefs and practices associated with sweet potato cultural management in Bukidnon, Philippines. In 1991, at the annual meeting of the International Potato Center in Southeast Asia, scientists from various disciplines were asked to comment on these indigenous beliefs and practices (for a fuller list of comments, see appendix E). The other columns of table 3.4 summarize scientific evaluations and comments by different scientists (one scientist representing each discipline). This is by no means exhaustive or representative of "the scientific stand," but it reveals interesting commonalities and differences of perspective between farmers and scientists, and even among scientists themselves, with respect to cultural management practices.

One thing that is obvious from an examination of column 1 is the adaptive value of indigenous knowledge in terms of the total agricultural system. For example, ginger, which has quite a pungent odor, is being effectively used as a weevil repellent; peanut, with its nitrogen-fixing property, is utilized for intercropping; and clearing the field of grasses that shelter competitors is practiced as a means of weed and pest control. Several scientists agreed with the soundness of these practices, a few of them going to the extent of elaborating the scientific bases of such practices.

It is also notable that some scientists have the ability to see beyond differences in terminology and phraseology to understand the reason behind practices. One local practice, of leaving insects alone because to "touch" them would only make things worse, may appear on the surface as irrational or superstitious. However, an entomologist explained that such a belief could prevent people from inadvertently killing "friendly insects" along with the not-so-friendly ones, thus upsetting the ecological balance of the farming system and doing more harm than good. Permitting the survival of beneficial insects is, of course, one of the basic tenets of integrated pest management (IPM). Likewise, the local belief that grasses, leaves, and other organic matter should be included with planting materials was justified by many of the scientists interviewed as a way to improve the texture, fertility, and overall quality of the soil.

This is not to say that all scientists have the perceptivity to appreciate the practical value and sound bases of farmer knowledge. The comments "scientifically unsound," "purely fanatic," "nonsense," and "foolish" are interspersed with scientific explanations validating farmers' agricultural beliefs and practices. The frequency of "no comment," "it depends," and "won't do any harm," however, may signify either an ingrained scientific ethic of suspending judgment until further verificatory study or a condescending attitude toward local beliefs and practices.

To return to the thesis that was presented earlier, there are several points of convergence between scientific knowledge and indigenous knowledge. The former, earlier referred to as the "science of the abstract" following Lévi-Strauss, in fact, hopes for tangible applications and must meet very concrete tests. On the other hand, indigenous knowledge—or the "science of the concrete"—is in fact based on quite sophisticated abstractions. Moreover, in both, redundancy is used to secure critical relationships or important outcomes. For instance, looking over table 3.4, it will be noted that many of the practices are working toward the same goal, be it soil enrichment or pest control. In the same way, scientific solutions are generally designed with a series of backup systems such that if one line of defense fails, there is another alternative or approach to buffer the system from collapse. A third point of convergence is the perceived necessity for, and the actual practice of, replication in both scientific trials and farmer trials. While this may not be so obvious in the latter case, farmers actually set aside small portions of their field for trying out innovations and compare the observed results with performance in "untreated controls." In addition, they compare notes with other farmers who have also tried the innovation or the treatment, as well as with those who have not. Lastly, within their own fields, farmers make detailed observations over a span of time, sometimes even intergenerationally, and therefore approximate "vertical" replication.

Much has been written about the value of local farming techniques for agricultural research and development (Brokensha et al. 1982; Fujisaka 1992;

TABLE 3.4 Scientists' Evaluations of Indigenous Agricultural Knowledge Pertaining to Sweet Potato Cultivation in Bukidnon, Philippines

Indigenous Cultural Management Beliefs and Practices	Scientific Evaluations and Comments by Discipline				
	Plant Pathologist	Entomologist	Agronomist	Plant Breeder	Plant Physiologist
Grasses and leaves are burned and the ashes are mixed with the cuttings so there will be many roots.	Ashes provide phosphorus which enhances tuber formation.	Organic fertilizer.	Ashes probably provide some nutrients at planting.	Ashes contain minerals.	No comment.
Ginger and peanuts are mixed with the planting materials for weevil resistance and for good harvest, respectively.	Ginger may be weevil-repellant and inter-cropping is a method of pest control.	Peanut can fix nitrogen thus increase yield; peanut and ginger act as insect repellant.	No comment.	Needs to be verified.	No comment.
Holy water is mixed with some cuttings so God will watch over and protect the crop.	Purely fanatic.	No comment.	No comment.	Water will be good for cuttings.	No comment.
Males should plant and should be naked so the harvest will be good.	Foolish!	No comment.	No comment.	No comment.	No comment.
Chemicals are not used, especially for sweet potatoes.	Depends!	Chemicals are too expensive considering the low price of sweet potatoes.	Depends on the kind; if indigenous fertilizers are used, plants grow more vines and leaves.	Chemical fertilizers have long-term negative effects on the environment.	Sweet potatoes are not as sensitive as other crops to pests and diseases; hence, no need for chemicals.

Grasses and weeds are cut using a scythe or long-bladed knife to maintain cleanliness of the area.	Sound.	Weeds compete for light, nutrients, and water.	This minimizes competition for light, nutrients, and water.	The farmer has little choice.	If farmer has enough resources to clear the area then he should; if not, the plants will not be terribly affected.
While weeding, trim off tops of plants so these will have more roots and will not die easily.	Trimming is a kind of stress which induces the plant to produce fruit/tuber to perpetuate its species.	Pruning sweet potato plants will increase yield depending on the volume of leaves removed.	Depends on the timing; probably good when done early and when growth is too luxuriant.	No comment.	No comment.
Rats are left alone because they cannot eat everything anyway.	Sweet potato is a low-income crop so use of pesticide will just increase cost of production and reduce return on investment.	No comment.	Chemical control is expensive and dangerous.	No comment.	No comment.
Allow insects and other pests to eat as much as they can because if they are "touched" they will become angry and damage everything in the field.	Nonsense!	Allow insects to "be" because some of them serve as biological control.	No comment.	No comment.	No comment.
Prayers are said to the gods (e.g., the god of rats) to implore them to spare/protect one's fields.	Nonsense!	No comment.	No comment.	Won't do any harm.	No comment.

Note: A more complete list of scientists' evaluations of indigenous beliefs and practices can be found in appendix E.

Sperling 1992). It is in fact currently fashionable—in other words, politically correct—to criticize science for its ostensibly objective, overly empirical approach (Chambers 1990a; Bentley and Andrew 1991; Johannsen 1992). In particular, agricultural science has come under fire for neglecting adaptations that have fostered the long-term survival of farming populations despite limited resources. The next constructive step is to seriously analyze the interface between agricultural science and indigenous knowledge, and to study how local perspectives and strategies can be effectively and fruitfully integrated into ongoing research and development. Central to the operationalization of indigenous knowledge systems in formal agricultural projects would be the search for points of negotiation between Western science and ethnoscience.

In this chapter, I have discussed the distribution and patterning of indigenous knowledge in relation to plant genetic resources, specifically sweet potatoes, and to agricultural development in general. The local histories of Intavas and Salvacion illustrate that a complex of factors precipitates commercialization of crop production. This includes, in the case of Salvacion, a particular history of migration, evolution of land tenure arrangements, and accessibility of market systems. Commercialization subsequently predisposes farmers to reorient criteria pertinent to the crop being produced so that characteristics that have a direct bearing on the salability of the crop—e.g., palatability, growth habits, and functional value—are given emphasis. Moreover, with market integration there develops a more pronounced divergence between males and females, as reflected in the latter's use of finer discrimination among sweet potato traits.

Extending the analysis further, I have attempted to demonstrate that there are important points of convergence—as well as divergence—between farmers' and scientists' evaluations of indigenous knowledge and practices. The question that needs to be asked, I think, is to what extent can farmers exert or even recognize their own priorities in making decisions about what crops or varieties to plant and what repertoire of knowledge and skills should be called to bear in nurturing these preferences? It is a legitimate concern for people interested in plant genetic resources because of the very real connection between biological and cultural diversity and the destabilizing effects of commercialization on this interface. Fortunately, I would argue, the system possesses a certain degree of resilience largely because of its fuzziness and marginality. I explore these aspects of resistance and irreverence to the hegemony of monoculture in the subsequent chapters.

4

IN DEFENSE OF FUZZINESS

The Value of Multiple Criteria

In chapter 3, we investigated the differentiation of evaluation criteria pertaining to varieties and technologies as a function of commercialization and modernization. The shift in focus of attention and script as farmers embrace hybrid varieties, Western technologies, and cash cropping could result in the erosion of landraces and local knowledge. There is one tenacious aspect of farmer decision making, however, that so far has served as an effective antidote against the wholesale abandonment of folk varieties and wisdom. I refer to the multiplicity of farmers' evaluation criteria regarding crops and agricultural technologies, as demonstrated here for sweet potatoes and their cultivation.

Although scientists initiate and contribute significantly to formal germplasm conservation programs, the key protagonists in any conservation effort are the farmers themselves, who nurture, propagate, and select the different varieties, as well as the agricultural knowledge and practices associated with the varieties' cultivation. In an effort to systematically document local adaptations and evaluation criteria, life histories of male and female farmers were elicited and analyzed with respect to their experiences in planting and consuming different varieties of sweet potatoes, the evolution of these practices and preferences, and the changes perceived regarding the diversity and composition of sweet potato varieties in the area. From the results of farmer interviews and participant observation, a file of indigenous beliefs and practices associated with each stage of the agricultural cycle has been constructed (appendix A). The above methods, coupled with more structured triads tests, also yielded a file of local evaluation criteria for sweet potatoes (appendix D).

DIVERSITY OF AGRICULTURAL BELIEFS AND PRACTICES

The indigenous technologies and beliefs associated with sweet potato cultivation in Bukidnon are summarized in table 4.1. Even a brief perusal of this table reveals the great diversity of agricultural decision making pertaining to sweet potatoes. There are, for example, different—frequently contradictory—beliefs and practices regarding the planting schedule, the source and spacing of planting materials, and the gender of the one who should do the planting. The same is true for nearly all stages of sweet potato production. At first, I thought that one of the interesting challenges that lay ahead was to find a way to reconcile the divergent beliefs and practices with a few underlying variables. As we (the members of the research team) spent more time in the field, however, it became more and more apparent that reconciling the differences in terms of any simplistic adaptive framework was out of the question. People retain a diversity of beliefs and practices, alternately hedging—following many, even at times conflicting, prescriptions to spread out the risks—and experimenting in an effort to find a match among varieties and technologies that work *most successfully most of the time*.

To illustrate further, farmers subscribe to different ideas of "things to mix" with planting materials (usually three sweet potato cuttings per hill) to induce better growth and greater productivity. In Intavas, people use cuttings of trees that have many thorns, as well as cuttings of plants with many roots. The belief behind the practice is that the numerous thorns, or roots as the case may be, will promote prolific root production in the sweet potato plants. A broom might also be included by some for this purpose. Together with grasses and leaves that are routinely included, these "metaphorical aids," when decomposed, serve as organic fertilizers, thus encouraging more vigorous plant growth and higher yield. In Salvacion, farmers include a tightly woven mat so the sweet potatoes will cluster instead of spreading out, a salamander so the roots will be big and long, and ashes from the kitchen stove so the sweet potatoes will have the desired powdery texture. Again, the value of these materials—tangible templates, in a sense—in improving both the texture and the organic content of the soil cannot be discounted.

The timing of planting sweet potatoes is another aspect that illustrates both expediency and an internal logic that facilitates adaptation. The most popular month for planting sweet potatoes in Bukidnon is November. The reason for this varies from traditional practice to simple market considerations. According to legend, the first sweet potato plant grew on the grave of a local maiden who had died from starvation because her parents refused to cook the grains they were saving to use as seeds for the next planting season. To comfort her parents, who were mourning her death, the daughter appeared to them in a dream and promised that she would send them a vine that produced an edible root every time it touched the ground. She did, and her parents carefully transplanted the first sweet potato plant from her grave to their field, later sharing the cuttings with their neighbors. To commemorate her magnanimous gesture, people have planted sweet potatoes on All Souls' Day (November 1). The other belief that brings about the same effect is that when one plants sweet potatoes in November there will be as many roots at harvest time as there are heads in the cemetery on the Day of the Dead.

On the more pragmatic side, November signals the end of the rainy season in Bukidnon and the onset of cooler weather. Planting during this period means less photosynthetic energy deflected to vegetative growth, less likelihood that the roots will rot from being waterlogged, and less risk that they will be attacked by insects and other pests that thrive during the warm and humid summer months. In terms of economic advantages, planting in November means that the roots will be harvestable in March or April, when they command a higher price because of the peak in demand with the approach of school graduation, vacation, and summer festivities.

Pest control practices also tend to cover all fronts. The most common sweet potato pests in Intavas and Salvacion are weevils and rats. The beliefs and practices aimed at their control revolve around sacred rites, such as beseeching the King of Rats to spare one's field, making offerings of food to the underground spirits to ask them to protect one's crops, and praying to the Almighty for divine intercession. Traditional practices, such as placing ginger on the soil so its strong, pungent odor will drive away pests, are also followed. One sees in these indigenous management practices—both sacred and secular—the scientific principles of attracting pests away from crops

TABLE 4.1. Indigenous Technologies and Beliefs Associated with Sweet Potatoes

Stage in Agricultural Cycle	Factor Considered	Prescriptions/Proscriptions
Land preparation	Material for tools	Metal implements may be used for land preparation but never for harvesting.
Planting	Lunar cycle	Plant during the first quarter so that the sweet potatoes will "bloom," or develop well.
		Plant during the full moon so that the tubers will be large.
		Plant during the last quarter so it will be relatively dark and insects won't attack the crop.
	Spacing	Cuttings should be well spaced so that the roots won't be overcrowded; permits tuber development.
		In planting different varieties in one's home garden, plant them apart to give each a chance to develop before they intertwine and mix.
	Planting technique	Bite the vines at several points before planting so that there will be many roots and tubers.
		Shape vines into a circle in planting so it will be easy to find the tubers later on.
	Gender of the one who plants	Females should plant the sweet potatoes so that the ground will crack later (indicating big tubers).
		Females should not plant sweet potatoes or else the tubers will crack.
		Males should plant so that tubers will be long.
		Males should plant naked in the dark so that the sweet potatoes will be prolific.
"Fertilizing"	Soil enrichment	Gather grass from under one's house and mix this with the soil and planting to improve the yield.

Category	Subcategory	Description
Pest management	Control of "worms" and "bugs"	Before planting, gather all caterpillars in one place and burn. Don't broil or roast the first harvest of sweet potatoes so as not to encourage pest infestation. Just boil them. Planting should be done when the moon is on the wane so insects won't see the sweet potatoes.
Harvesting	Tools	Never harvest with metal implements, as these will damage the developing tubers. Use only wooden/bamboo implements or hands for picking mature tubers.
	Method	Harvesting should be done on a staggered basis (big ones first) so there will be no storage problems and there will always be some left for future needs.
	Gender of harvester	First harvest should not be done by males or they will turn into wild animals.
Storage	Post-harvest handling of tubers	Dry tubers in the sun so they will "ripen," and then store under heaps of dried grass. Don't wash tubers so they won't rot. Wash them just before eating. Store tubers in special bamboo baskets (buda) so they will keep longer. To make sweet potato last even longer, chop and dry to make chips. These will keep for months.

A more complete list of indigenous beliefs and practices can be found in appendix A.

through decoys and driving them away through fumigation. And the results are probably as effective as modern techniques, thus reinforcing the practices.

The prescriptions also include practical cultural management practices, like cleaning the area so there will be no hiding and breeding places for pests; diversionary tactics, like setting up waving cellophane strips on bamboo poles to scare away the rats; and direct modes of attack, like installing handcrafted rat traps in the sweet potato fields. When all else fails, farmers maintain their composure by rationalizing that neither rats nor weevils can consume the entire crop and that there will always be some left for people to consume. This "live and let live" attitude—a very sound indigenous interpretation of the principle of ecological balance—sees the farmers through hard times and, I believe, contributes significantly to the sustainability of their farming systems.

I have tried to coax the fan of strategies into a more serious, orthodox framework, but none seems to fit better or provide greater explanatory power given the results than the "framework" of expediency and fuzziness. By this I mean the evolution and persistence of technologies based on day-to-day pragmatic concerns and the natural inertia that preserves diversity based on demands that cannot be fully satisfied by any one "ideal" or "best" variety or technology. Rather than detract from the significance of adaptation, expediency and fuzziness simply emphasize the often neglected importance of unplanned, unsought, and underappreciated factors in influencing the direction—or directions—adaptation will take.

HETEROGENEITY OF INDIGENOUS EVALUATION CRITERIA

From casual interviews, participant observation, and the results of life history elicitation, the common local descriptors of sweet potatoes were gleaned and compiled. Table 4.2 summarizes the important features and parameters for characterizing sweet potato varieties in Bukidnon, with Tagalog and English translations. On the one hand, it reveals the extent of variation recognized; on the other, it demonstrates the degree of sensory refinement and observational skill and effort that have gone into the descriptions.

In addition to local description, the local basis for distinguishing among sweet potato varieties was investigated using triads test and informal interviews, as discussed in the previous chapter. It may be recalled that when male and female farmers were asked to discriminate among sets of three sweet potato

TABLE 4.2. Local Descriptions of Sweet Potato Features

Important Features	Binukid Adjectives	Tagalog Adjectives	Cebuano Adjectives	English Adjectives
Color of flesh	maputi	puti	puti	white
	makalawag	dilaw	dalag	yellow
	maitum	maitim	itum	black (dark)
	ubihon	ube	ubihon	violet
	maliga	pula	pula	red
Color of skin	makalawag	dilaw	dalag	yellow
	maputi	puti	puti	white
	pink	rosas	pink	pink
	pula	pula	pula	red
	brown	tsokolate	brown	brown
Shape of leaves	gireng-gireng	gahi-gahi	gireng-gireng	serrated
	pino	pino	pino	fine
Flesh texture	madabo	mayabo	dabo/labo	dry
	malunay	basa	malunay	watery
	gamiton	maugat	ugaton	fibrous
Taste	tab-ang	matabang	tab-ang	bland
	maumis	matamis	tam-is	sweet
	maumis	masarap	lame	delicious
Shape of roots	lidong-lidong	pabilog	lingin	roundish
	malayat	pahaba	tag-as or taas	elongated
	balugto	liku-liko or balikuko	baliko	irregular
Size of roots	atiyo	maliit	gamay	small
	arage	malaki	dako	large
Number of roots	mabunga	mabunga	maunod	prolific
	hari mabunga	hindi mabunga	dili maunod	not productive
Saleability of roots	halinon	mabili	palitunun	highly saleable
	dili halinon	matumal	dili palitunun	not saleable
Weevil infestation	buntiyakon	may tanga	bukbukon	infested
	hari buntiyakon	walang tanga	walay bukbok	not infested

varieties and to state the criteria they used in distinguishing among varieties, the criteria they employed were diverse and far from mutually exclusive. Morphological, gastronomic, life habit, familiarity, and functional criteria were used simultaneously, albeit with differing frequency based on the degree of market integration and gender of the informant (see table 3.5 and figure 3.5).

The diversity of local descriptors and evaluation criteria supports the contention that selection and adoption of varieties and of technologies are not unilinear processes that involve a purposive elimination of "less fit" or "less desirable" options. Analysis of informal interviews indicates that what is desirable and what is not is really a matter of taste, a matter of timing, and sometimes even a matter of mood. In other words, agricultural decision making may not be a question of the systematic evaluation of alternatives but more of "muddling through" or examining by trial and error the various options that are perceived to be available and accessible, reflecting what Keesing (1987:383) referred to as "a partial and situational *ad hoc* quality of folk models." Moreover, like indigenous agricultural beliefs and practices, local criteria for the evaluation of sweet potato varieties tend to be fuzzy or to trail off into gray areas as to which properties or traits are positive or preferred and which ones are negative or not preferred.

Table 4.3 summarizes some of these characteristics and identifies the sources of fuzziness, or "gray areas." It is quite clear from this table that there is not one variety that can possibly satisfy all the desires of the sweet potato farmers and/or consumers. The following comment from an elderly female farmer in Bukidnon corroborated this observation: "I plant several varieties instead of just one so that we can choose. For example, the bland variety is good in combination with dried fish. If it is sweet, I would easily get satiated. Powdery and bland varieties are good for combining with meat and soup, wet and sweet ones go well with coffee, and sweet and powdery ones are preferred by children for snacks, although often disliked by adults because the dryness sometimes makes them choke."

In Salvacion, where due to market demands many farmers primarily plant a variety called *kasindol*, several farmers still devote a few rows on the margins of commercial plots to the cultivation of different varieties of sweet potatoes for home consumption. These rows contain varieties too bland for the market but that make good rice substitutes, somewhat bitter varieties with medicinal properties, varieties with roots that are too small to be marketable but that are sweet and dry, nonproductive varieties by economic and agronomic standards but prolific producers of leaves that are good for salads, and

TABLE 4.3. Gray Areas in Local Evaluation Criteria

| Criteria | Categories | | Fuzziness |
	Normally Preferred	Normally Not Preferred	
Texture	dry/powdery	wet/watery	*but* dry varieties can cause choking and easily crack when cooked (therefore, not good for *camote cue*)
Taste	sweet	bland	*but* sweet varieties make one easily satiated; bland ones are a better substitute for rice, and are also used as thickening for soup
Digestibility	easy to digest	hard to digest	*but* hard-to-digest varieties are more "stomach filling," so it takes longer for one to feel hungry again
Size of roots	big	small	*but* some big ones are tasteless while many small ones are tasty; also, those varieties with big roots tend to have fewer roots
Use	produce edible roots	do not produce edible roots	*but* some of those without edible roots produce better-tasting leaves or leaves with greater medicinal value
Familiarity	traditional	new	*but* although traditional varieties are more delicious, they take too long to mature.

the like. A comment by one of the female farmers in Salvacion was particularly instructive: "I plant whatever sells well in the market, but at the margins around the rows I plant different kinds. Let me tell you. The sweet ones with dry texture are for the market because they command a good price. The sweet ones that are watery are for our snacks. The bland, dry kind is a good substitute for bread and rice. And the bland, wet ones are for the pigs."

A different set of concerns was reflected in this remark from a male farmer from Salvacion: "I ask for different planting materials from our neighbors, but I don't mix them up. I plant at least five different varieties of sweet potatoes at any one time to experiment from which ones I can get the most benefit. At different seasons, we should plant different varieties because we never know which ones would be the most productive."

This practice is even more prevalent in Intavas, where the different varieties are not segregated in neat rows but are interspersed in small clumps from which the farmer can easily pick the variety he or she wants to consume at any particular time. The following comments from Intavas farmers provide a window into their decision-making framework:

> We plant different varieties so we can have different tastes. When we have coffee, we eat the bland ones. When we have only water to drink, we pick the sweet ones. If we don't have the appetite for one kind, then we use the other kind. We never get hungry.

> Traditional varieties are small but sweet. We plant different kinds. With different varieties, one has a choice. If you get tired of dry, powdery ones, then you can harvest the wet kind. If you get tired of sweet ones, then you can have the bland ones.

The above observations lead me to think that diversity is actually the natural state of things—almost, although not quite, assured by the multiplicity of criteria for sweet potato preferences for different occasions, different seasons, and for different kinds of farmers. If it were not for these stabilizing mechanisms, landraces and associated agricultural knowledge would have vanished from farmers' fields—and minds—a long time ago. Nevertheless, the natural pull toward diversity, while robust, is not indestructible. It should be protected as much as possible by policies geared to the preservation of biodiversity and farming systems or agro-ecosystems that nurture crop diversity. Ideally, it should also be reinforced by economic incentives for mixed or diverse produce and social recognition and/or economic subsidies for farmers who continue cultivating landraces and heirloom varieties.

MUDDLING THROUGH TO DIVERSITY

A careful examination of the data on indigenous technologies and local evaluation criteria among farmers in Bukidnon has led me to question whether we can ever fit the data into neat paradigms such as Gladwin's (1980) decision tree model or Rosch's (1978) graded structures. In the former, decision making is visualized as proceeding through a series of hierarchal alternatives, represented as branching yes/no nodes and internodes. The decision maker supposedly goes through the sequence of discrete decision-making criteria until he or she reaches the final resolution and an outcome or choice is made. By contrast, the theory of graded structures postulates that natural or culturally relevant categories invariably have a graded structure. Hence, examples falling under a particular category can be "arranged" in a gradient with respect to the "goodness of fit" with the prototype that best represents the category to those whose membership in the category is marginal or fuzzy. Using this conceptual framework, for example, a teacup may be considered as a prototypical cup because it measures up to every idealized aspect of "cupness," whereas a mug, because it is big and flat-bottomed, is more of a marginal member of the category. This implies that the evaluation of whether a certain sweet potato variety is an ideal representative or a peripheral inclusion in the category "desirable to plant" or "desirable to eat" is determined by the degree of its conformity to certain specified and required characteristics.

From the results of this study, we can see that decision making does not proceed through a sequential resolution of dyadic alternatives as in Gladwin's decision tree model. Based on observed evaluation criteria, a *hypothetical* model of a decision tree pertaining to choice of a sweet potato variety is presented in figure 4.1. However, I have yet to encounter a farmer who systematically evaluates his or her options in this manner. Instead, the criteria are considered together and perceived in a gestalt manner so that varieties may be retained not because they possess all the desirable attributes (or score a "yes" on all the nodes) but because there are *compensatory* traits that make their cultivation worthwhile. There is apparently no need to sell the idea of maintaining diversity to small-scale farmers, the inertia or pull being in this direction. We have only to refrain from contributing to hegemonic forces (including narrow and shortsighted economic, political, and technological agendas) that can overpower and reverse a natural adaptive tendency.

This brings us to a bind with respect to conventional systems of crop improvement and technology generation. In agricultural research and development efforts, there is an understandable search for the prototype—a quest for the ideal—whether one is talking about technologies or about crops. What is the best kind and concentration of fertilizers? When is the best time to initiate pest control measures? Which is the best variety of rice, corn,

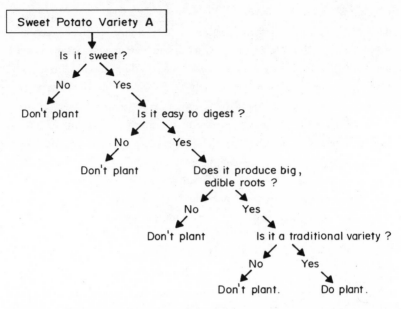

Figure 4.1. Hypothetical decision tree on whether to plant variety A of sweet potato, following Gladwin.

wheat, or sweet potato? It goes without saying that it is easier to package agricultural recommendations when these can be streamlined, with fuzziness reduced to a minimum. Unfortunately, this demand for parsimony in the name of efficiency and productivity often also entails an unwarranted reductionism that can do more harm than good by closing our eyes to the infinitely interesting array of interacting and complicating factors.

It is, I think, a counterproductive waste of energy, from the point of view of user-sensitive agricultural development, to strive to design and promote *the* technology or *the* variety that is supposed to work or to be desirable under all (or almost all) circumstances. In the first place, farmer resistance and/or apathy will be considerable, if not overwhelming. Secondly, the ramifications could backfire in terms of loss of diversity—both genetic and cultural. The most we can do is to try to preserve existing options, offer what we believe are the best alternatives after we have struggled to see through farmers' eyes, and trust the farmers to "muddle through" to their best interest. I think we will be surprised at how inspired and insightful the muddling-through process is in the final analysis, forged as it has been in the most trying of circumstances.

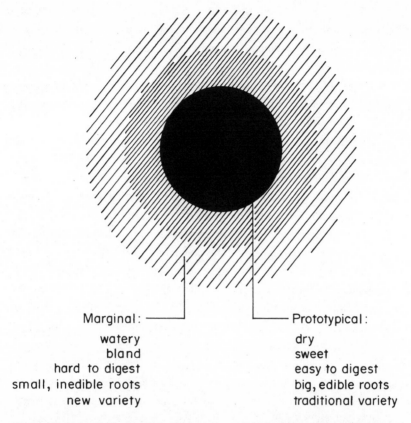

Marginal: ————┐   ┌———— Prototypical:

watery	dry
bland	sweet
hard to digest	easy to digest
small, inedible roots	big, edible roots
new variety	traditional variety

Figure 4.2. Hypothetical model of the category "ideal sweet potato variety," following Rosch's theory of graded structures.

In reality, it is difficult to construe the "prototypical" or ideal sweet potato variety (fig. 4.2) because people also look for and maintain the more "marginal" characteristics in their sweet potato stock. Hence, there is no unilinear gradient on which we can arrange sweet potato varieties from the most desirable or "ideal" to those that are progressively less so, *if* we make farmers' evaluation criteria paramount. As one farmer succinctly put it, "We plant different varieties so that if we are fed up with one, we can try another. . . . It is just like the case of clothes. You choose the ones you like for the day." This is the reason why the farmers of Bukidnon easily empathize with the problem of genetic erosion, citing some delicious or prolific varieties that were "lost" and lamenting the fact they can no longer find planting materials for these varieties. Nevertheless, research on local criteria does reveal the *kind* of features that farmers consider important—in this case, morphological and gastronomic rather than agronomic and functional—and thus may lead us to fruitfully challenge fundamental assumptions in scientific plant breeding and conservation.

In this section, I have reported many instances wherein choice is influenced by multiple considerations that impinge on farmers' decision making, simultaneously and synergistically leading to hedging, compromise, and, fortuitously, the maintenance of biodiversity in local farming communities. The balance, however, is precarious and, as in any open system, can be disturbed by external influences ranging from extension to commercialization to legislation. Given the snowballing effect of modernization and the concomitant simplification and homogenization of agriculture, it is inspiring to note the inherent penchant of farmers for diversity and the fact that, for reasons that make sense, they are safeguarding this diversity.

The problem is when fuzzy, adaptive local perceptions that foster diversity collide with the ordering, reductionistic principles of formal science, be it agronomic or economic in nature. Kosko pinpointed this dissonance in a more general vein: "I called this the *mismatch problem: The world is gray but science is black and white.* We talk in zeroes and ones but the truth lies in between. Fuzzy world, nonfuzzy descriptions. The statements of formal logic and computer programming are all true or false, 1 or 0. But statements about the world differ. . . . They are not bivalent but multivalent, gray, fuzzy" (1993:8; italics added).

If we are willing to tolerate a certain degree of uncertainty and complexity, and to suspend our favorite abstractions and dichotomies for a while, we can see that actually agricultural decision making does not proceed (and, I suspect, never has proceeded) through a neat series of nodes and internodes. Nor is there a central concept, or cultural notion, as to what an ideal or best variety or technology is. The questions that always follow, minimally, are, Best when? Best for what? Best for whom? Moreover, the questions are apparently handled iteratively rather than sequentially, with considerations being given different weights according to farmers' individual situations and perceptions. That there is no one answer for any of these questions is probably the best deterrent against the loss of diversity in farmers' fields and memories.

5

THREATENED POCKETS
OF MEMORIES

Diversity at the Margins

Genes and cultures have something very important in common: both are repositories of coded information essential to adaptation and survival. More than this, genetic information and cultural information co-evolve in the sense that directions and latitudes set in one sphere inevitably shape constraints and choices in the other sphere. The Green Revolution and biotechnology are but two of the most recent and dramatic demonstrations of how cultural change, motivated by a Baconian creed coupled with boundless faith in the "technological fix," affects genetic variability, which in turn limits (some would contend that it expands) the options available to farming populations integrated into the market economy or the world system.

With the hegemonic trend in agricultural development emphasizing high productivity, short maturity, and input sensitivity in both crops and technology, genetic information coded in wild strains and farmers' landraces is threatened with erosion and eventual loss. Likewise, cultural practices or indigenous knowledge and technologies associated with traditional varieties are in imminent danger of being swamped by modern technology. Hence, given the tight interlinkages between human intervention and biotic diversity in all but the simplest of agro-ecological systems, a piecemeal approach to conservation is no longer sufficient. This was recognized in 1992 by the World Resources Institute and its collaborators in drafting the *Global Biodiversity Strategy*. In endorsing one of the ten principles for conserving biodiversity, the *Strategy* asserted that "cultural diversity is closely linked to biodiversity.

Humanity's collective knowledge of biodiversity and its use and management rests in cultural diversity. Conversely, conserving biodiversity often helps strengthen cultural integrity and values" (23).

It may be recalled that the initial reconnaissance and benchmark survey of the two areas showed less diversity in Salvacion than in Intavas in terms of the actual number of sweet potato varieties cultivated, as well as in the number of varieties known but not actually cultivated. More important, we have seen from table 3.2 that there is a significantly narrower discrepancy in terms of actual crop diversity than in terms of cognized crop diversity, indicating a faster rate of attrition of agricultural knowledge than of genetic diversity itself. Fortunately, it is increasingly appreciated that narrowing the genetic and cultural base of any population predisposes that population to instabilities and makes it more vulnerable to ecological and social stress. This is the driving force behind the establishment of gene banks and also the rationale for memory banking. It may not be as widely recognized, however, that farmers at the margins—or those who by virtue of their subsistence orientation, distance from markets, and/or lesser degree of integration with centralized political hierarchies are more sheltered from agricultural commercialization—retain more of their knowledge as *pockets of memories* about technologies, as well as retaining the landraces themselves. As has been demonstrated in chapter 4, a significant contributing factor in this retention could be the prevailing multiplicity of local evaluation criteria or fuzziness of decision making pertaining to varietal choice.

A COMMERCIAL AND SUBSISTENCE FARMER: DEGREES OF INTEGRATION AND RESISTANCE

By pockets of memories I refer to more or less persistent cognitive schemas regarding the evaluation, cultivation, and consumption of traditional crops. These memories are "threatened" in the sense that in order for farmers to survive in a changing world, they also have to be cognizant of, and respond to, external developments brought about by changes in policy, markets, and agricultural research and extension. Sometimes this means giving up landraces and agricultural beliefs and practices that they valued in the past to make way for new cultivars and more modern technologies in order to compete effectively in the larger world or simply to avail themselves of its credit and extension infrastructure.

Yet there are degrees of protection afforded by distance and independence. Just as adaptive radiation and edge effect have always flourished in ecotones, and ecological diversity has invariably been favored in ecosystems characterized by little or no dominance, so farmers who find themselves in what we would characterize as marginal situations stand a better chance of retaining more of their options in their minds, and most likely in their fields as well (see appendixes A and D). They are in a sense spared from what has been referred to as "roadside development." In this section I present the life histories of two male farmers: the first is a semicommercial sweet potato grower in Salvacion; the second is a native Bukidnon who cultivates sweet potatoes mainly for subsistence.

> My name is Melencio Avergonzado. I was born in the year 1932, in Bohol. When I was growing up, my parents planted several varieties of sweet potatoes, including *katuko, bunwanon, kabuko, banas,* and *tapol.* Myself, I was a *carabao* caretaker. We had plenty of carabaos then. I enjoyed doing this task because I was able to meet people my own age.
>
> Even when I was still young, I was already business-minded. I made guitars [*bagol*] while my friends were watching over the carabaos. I would sell them to my friends and acquaintances. I also constructed small plows [*tarian*]. I did not lose interest in business even as I grew up. I became a *manananggot* [a person who gathers *tuba,* a semifermented coconut wine, and sells it in the market]. I also sold bread, fish, and soft drinks. Some people were ashamed of selling fish and the like, but I was not ashamed of what I was doing. After World War II, when I was about twelve years old, I bought and sold pigs and chickens. I also went to Davao and planted cabbage and coffee. I wanted to become independent and be able to plan my future. I stayed in Davao for two years until I was forced to return to Bohol because my mother got sick. From then on, I helped my parents and stayed in Bohol until I got married.
>
> To earn a living after I got married, I engaged in several business ventures. In addition to tuba and coconut, I also marketed rice and fish; sometimes I would trade one type of goods for another. Our life was difficult during those times, but I worked very hard for us

to survive. We were very poor and had many children. I decided then to move to Mindanao and take the risk. I only waited for my eight children to grow a little older before we traveled to this place. Here, I began to plant a sweet potato variety called *kasindol*. It is the most preferred variety in this place because it produces many roots. I always make it a point to cultivate this crop, and I also encouraged my children and my neighbors to plant it because I knew this would bail us out of our poverty. They followed my suggestion, and as you can see, we have vast land planted to sweet potato here at Salvacion. Some are making a profit by selling the produce at the market in Agusan Canyon. The other varieties of sweet potato we have right now are *binawon, amerikano, klarin*, and *initlog*. The largest area is the one devoted to kasindol. It has greater value, for it produces many roots. This variety came from Bohol.

Based on experience, we follow several practices in cultivating sweet potatoes. First of all, the area should be well cleaned and the soil should be properly cultivated. We have a belief that the right time for planting is during full moon and low tide. The explanation of the elders was that during low tide, many rocks and stones can be seen, so likewise sweet potato will produce many roots. Sometimes we also go by the days of the week. We do not plant when the day has the letter "r," like Martes [Tuesday]. To do so is to court bad luck. Instead, we plant on Sabado [Saturday] because there is no "r" in the name. It is also said that there are articles that are associated with good harvest. Since I am the one who knows about these, I am the one who plants. If the area is flat, we use the plow, but if the area is sloping, we use a long, sharp knife or *bolo*. We do not use the plow in sloping land, to prevent soil erosion. We hire laborers when we have money [₱25.00/day/person], but most of the time the family members do all the farming tasks. It will just add to the expenses of the family if we hire laborers.

In planting sweet potato, the tops should be cut every time they grow, to preserve the planting materials. If you just let them grow, there is a risk that they will die and you will not retain cuttings for planting. Those vines that are cut should be planted immediately. If there are rodents or other pests, we do not use chemicals to control them. We just maintain the cleanliness of the area, and the sweet potatoes will not be attacked by the rodents. This is true even with corn.

With regard to harvesting, we use a wooden stick to prevent any damage to vines and roots that are not yet ready for harvesting. Damaging the vines and roots may stop further development of the younger roots under the ground. When there are a lot of harvested roots, especially during summer, we peel the skin, then slice or chop the roots into small pieces and dry them under the sun. This way we can store them for some months. Some roots are buried under the ground, but these will last only for a couple of weeks.

Among the varieties, I prefer kasindol because it produces many roots. Did you know that when we came here, we brought different varieties of sweet potato? But the others did not produce as many roots as the kasindol variety. Because of its high yield, it is more profitable to plant kasindol than to grow corn. When we sell it, it gives us enough money to buy rice. It can also be cooked as *camote cue* [sliced, fried, and sweetened sweet potatoes skewered on a bamboo stick], which is the favorite of the family. Kasindol is suited for this recipe for it does not crack when cooked. Sometimes, if we don't have any side dish, we mix sweet potato leaves with rice, especially the tender tops. We also dry the sliced sweet potato roots. It is a good "cure" for severe hunger pangs.

I am Sixto Mahayao, seventy-five years old. I was born and grew old in Intavas. When I was young, our source of livelihood was cultivating corn, sweet potato, cassava, and taro. We also planted abaca and coffee. We had a large plantation of abaca, but it was attacked by *alquires*, a kind of disease. Hence, the area planted for abaca became smaller.

When I was about ten years old, I always harvested abaca. This was our only source of cash for buying food. During those times, we suffered a lot because we were very poor and the war situation was not very good. The sweet potato that we planted during those days were *kauyag*, which has yellow skin and white flesh; *lamputi*, which has white leaves, skin, and flesh; *lawaton*, which has yellow skin and flesh; *manugyang*, which has yellow skin; *pas-ok*, which has red skin and yellow flesh; and *bul-ok*, which has red skin and yellow flesh.

Kabaring and *klarin* are also almost like bul-ok. The difference only lies on the leaves since both kabaring and klarin have fingerlike leaves. However, the leaves of klarin have red edges, while those of kabaring are all green. Manugyang, by contrast, is like *kalating*. It has yellow flesh and yellow skin, but the root is curved and elongated. *Turay* has dark skin, and its leaves are green with red stripes.

In addition to sweet potatoes, we also planted coffee, abaca, cassava, and taro. But these crops were only planted in small areas because we did not have a carabao. They were cultivated for home consumption only, except for coffee. Coffee served as our main source of income because the trees live for a long time. When coffee bore fruit, then we could eat rice because we had money to buy rice. When they did not bear fruit, we ate our corn, sweet potato, cassava, and taro as substitutes for rice.

Today, the varieties of sweet potatoes that we are planting are *lambayong, camba, si-uron*, and turay. We also have *gireng-gireng*, which produces tops and leaves that are good vegetables. We have chosen to cultivate different varieties so that we can have many choices.

Planting is done with the use of *bolo*. The bark of a tree—any kind of tree but preferably one with many branches—is mixed with the planting materials and a prayer is said. This practice encourages sweet potatoes to have as many roots as the number of the branches of the tree. The planting activity can be done by a male or a female so he or she can contribute to the income of the family. Full moon is the best time to plant so that the roots will be big. We always plant six vines to a hill, three in front and three at the sides, so that when one cutting dies, there are still others that will grow. Also, there will be many roots. However, I observed that while in the past years there were many roots produced, today there are only few. I cannot explain why.

We control pests by clearing the area and by tying cellophane strips or any light white material to bamboo poles in the different parts of the field. The waving strips frighten the rodents. Sometimes we also put some traps that we make ourselves.

Harvesting should be done using a stick to avoid damaging the roots. It is usually done with an offering, such as cooked eggs, along with prayers. Seven months is the maturity period for sweet potato.

Harvesting is done in a staggered manner. We harvest only when needed by the family, hence we don't store the roots. Because we use a stick instead of a knife or a hoe, we avoid damaging the remaining roots, so we always have something to harvest for the next season. We do all the work in the farm, and we do not use fertilizer or any chemicals for sweet potato.

The harvested roots are always broiled or boiled. Sometimes we also cook *tinabirak* [a kind of porridge] by peeling off the skin of the roots and slicing it into small pieces. The pieces are then placed in a kettle filled with water and left to boil until the desired texture is reached. The leaves are often used as vegetables. Some varieties like pas-ok can be used to cure *kubag* [skin disease]. The leaves will be placed over the fire and will be applied to the affected area. Lamputi is another variety that is good for a sick person. This is served as a vegetable. If we have excess harvest, we feed them to the pigs and chicken.

I myself like sweet potatoes that are powdery like kauyag and si-uron. These varieties are very satisfying and will not cause one to choke. Bland or tasteless varieties do not appeal to me. Sweet potato has helped us a lot, especially in times of poverty.

MARGINALITY'S ROLE IN THE CONSERVATION OF DIVERSITY

Although commercialization has made significant inroads in most farming communities, many farmers—including, to different degrees, Melencio Avergonzado and Sixto Mahayao—retain a subsistence orientation relative to at least a few crops such as sweet potatoes. Brush (1992) pointed out that the agro-climatic and social heterogeneity that characterize many marginal areas play an important role in restraining the diffusion of improved crop varieties. Speaking of the tendency of Third World farmers to maintain multiple-cropping systems that promote both inter- and intraspecific variation, Altieri and Merrick explained that this strategy promotes "diversity of diet and income source, stability of production, minimization of risk, reduced insect and disease incidence, efficient use of labor, intensification of production with limited resources, and maximization of returns under low levels of technology" (1987:88).

In chapter 3, I traced the reverberations of agricultural intensification in evaluation criteria and scripts of farmers and scientists and discussed the effect this may have on the diversity of agricultural crops and practices. The life histories included in this chapter further demonstrate the richness of knowledge that is threatened by full-scale commercialization of agricultural production. No "magic bullet" payoff from productionism—exemplified by "charts of data showing increased yields and output, and the declining share of consumer paychecks going to food expenditures on one hand, juxtaposed with particular 'big hit' technologies (e.g., hybrid corn, green-revolution rice and wheat varieties, DDT, artificial insemination) on the other" (Buttell 1993:6)—can compensate for the loss of this legacy.

The documentation of this invaluable heritage is an urgent task. But so is the need for societal reinforcement for the resistance of farmers to indiscriminate adoption engendered by wholesale commercialization and monoculture. Ian Deshmukh, in a commentary published in *Diversity*, pointed to this need: "The major practical problems of conservation are not biological but socioeconomic. . . . Until biological conservation becomes multi-disciplinary, its successes will be small or short-lived. Creative solutions are needed if present trends in biodiversity are to be slowed. Such solutions will involve knowledge and support of poor rural communities in developing countries. This support will not come from comprehension of biological principles, but from recognition and development of existing cultures and their use of biological resources" (1989:321).

A MIGRANT AND A NATIVE: TWO WOMEN TELL THEIR STORIES

Within the farming population itself, women are generally strategically situated by virtue of the cultural definition of their roles to perform the nurturing/perpetuating function—in other words, to serve as conduits of genetic and cultural transmission. The binary oppositions dominating the world view of many indigenous cultures, related as they are to sexual polarization, give some indication as to who performs what. For example, in most cultures the parallels to the *male/female* dichotomy include, among others, *dry/wet*, *hard/soft*, *infertile/fertile*, and *hot/cold*. From these parallel dyads, it can be seen that traits associated with femaleness (i.e., wet, soft, fertile, and cold) are also those associated with Mother Earth and most of her "lowly" creatures (see, for example, Rappaport 1968). In short, based on dominant symbolism, women are culturally expected to be caretakers or stewards of nature. On a more pragmatic plane, women as a rule are the cultivators of subsistence, as opposed to cash, crops because they have the responsibility of seeing that everyone in the household gets fed and cared for on a day-to-day basis. Women have traditionally fulfilled this expectation by gathering, cultivating, and trading food and medicinal crops. Therefore, their decisions with respect to resource use (including plant and animal resources) dominate in a sphere that is relatively insulated from pressures toward monoculture, commercialization, and technological change.

Two oral histories of women cultivators are presented to illustrate the vital role played by women in protecting and transmitting the genetic as well as the cultural heritage. The first woman is a native of Intavas; the second woman is a migrant from the Visayas who has settled in Salvacion.

My name is Elena Gayunan, and I am sixty-five years old. I was born near the Batugan River, in an area that is also part of Intavas. My parents have always planted sweet potatoes, and I got all my cuttings from them. Even when it is dry season and other crops refuse to grow or bear fruit, sweet potato can still thrive and produce roots. Thus, if we have nothing else to eat, we can always depend on this plant. In fact, we call it *tambal sa gutom*, or cure for hunger.

Although I am a native of this place, I have also experienced moving to different places around Mt. Kitanglad. When I turned sixteen, I lived with my cousin at Impalutao, Impasug-ong. Then I stayed in Claveria, Misamis Oriental, for one year. After I met my husband, we decided to go back to Intavas. We worked on my mother's land near Mt. Kitanglad. My whole life, I have always been farming: corn, sweet potato, and different kinds of root crops in Impasug-ong, and coffee, corn, and sweet potato here.

Here in Intavas, where we have to depend on the rain, we choose drought- and heat-resistant crops such as taro, corn, squash, and, of course, sweet potato. I have always helped my father to care for these plants because my mother died when I was still quite young. The sweet potato varieties that we cultivated during those days were *kauyag*, which has dirty white skin and flesh and red tops; *lawaton*, which has white skin, yellow flesh, and red tops; *camba*, which has red skin, yellow flesh, and big roots; *lambayong*, which has yellow skin and flesh and red tops; and *lamputi*, which has white skin, flesh, and leaves. Those I've described are the traditional varieties among us Bukidnons. In addition, we also grew *kulating, ganganon, dinagat,* and *kampol.* There are still others, but I've forgotten some of them.

Anyway, there are newer ones that we've also grown fond of. These are *initlog*, which has yellow skin, yellow powdery flesh like the yolk of an egg, and dark green vines; *si-uron*, which has red skin and white flesh; *meruga*, which has yellow flesh and red leaves; and *turay*, which has white skin, violet flesh, and white leaves. We plant different kinds of sweet potatoes so when we are fed up with one variety there are always others to choose from. You see, it is just like clothes, you choose the ones you like best at that particular moment. Elders like different varieties so they can choose the one that suits their taste or combines well with other items in their meal.

Clearing the land is done through slash-and-burn. Then a *bolo* is used to loosen the soil and plant the crops. When we plant sweet potato, we mix it with a plant called *karogom*, which is known for having many roots. The fruits of this plant are mixed with the planting materials of sweet potato—usually three cuttings per hill—so that the sweet potato will have as many roots as the karogom plant. Other people use dried grasses and leaves, which are plentiful in the area, to mix with planting materials. Sometimes the grasses and leaves are first burned and turned to ashes before mixing with the soil. It also helps if we plant during full moon so the roots will be big and numerous.

When it comes to harvesting, we do not use any metal implements like bolo or grab hoe. Instead, we use bamboo or wooden sticks. This way we do not damage the young roots or the vines. These will be covered with soil again after we harvest the big roots so the smaller sweet potatoes can continue growing. We believe that the first harvest should not be broiled because this would cause damage to the roots that remain in the field. The first harvest should instead just be boiled. Since we do not store sweet potatoes, we feed the excess harvest to our pigs and allow the rest to ripen for a week. After seven days, the sweet potatoes become sweet and delicious—unlike when they are newly harvested, when the taste is rather bland.

Essentially, we leave pests like weevil and rodents alone because anyway it is impossible for them to consume everything. Our elders used to offer roasted chicken with their prayers for the god of rats to protect their fields. But this practice is not commonly observed by the younger generation. The same is true with communal and exchange labor that was practiced extensively before but is now being replaced by hired labor. However, in my family, which is quite extended, all the members help except the small children. Sometimes we also ask for the help of other relatives and some neighbors. Many things have changed, but sweet potatoes have always seen us through hard times.

I am Concordia Gerong, born in 1917, in Maasin, Southern Leyte. Our parents died when I was still young, leaving my two brothers and myself to take care of each other. I worked as a housemaid while my brothers worked in the farm. We never went to school.

When I was seventeen, I got married. To earn a living for my family, I would go to the mountains to buy abaca from the natives, bring down the abaca (sometimes weighing as much as 1,000 kilos) by jeepney, and sell these to the merchants in town. It was hard work, but we prospered. I tried my best because I have many children, twenty-one in all. At one point I was also ferrying bamboo slats and banana leaves in addition to the abaca.

Farming has been another important source of livelihood from the time I was young to the time that I had a family of my own. We planted coconut, corn, rice, and many varieties of sweet potatoes. In Leyte we liked *karampag*, which has rounded roots with white skin and yellow flesh that is very dry and powdery; *tugabang*, which has pinkish, fingerlike leaves with red tender tops and yellow sweet flesh; *karunsing*, which has elongated roots with red skin and white flesh; *kabutho*, which has white skin and flesh and which tastes bland unless allowed to ripen for three days; *sinentabo*, which produces elongated roots during the first harvest but subsequently produces rounded roots; and *kalidades*, which has pink skin and flesh of many colors (pink, yellow, and white) and is very powdery in texture.

The first one who moved to Bukidnon in search of work was my eldest son. Later, I followed with my other three sons, and we settled here in Salvacion. The people in this place were used to planting corn but not sweet potato. But my family has always been planting sweet potatoes; for every piece of land we cultivate, we make it a point to allocate an area for sweet potatoes. We do this because we have many children and we can always depend on sweet potatoes to help us feed them. We kept this practice even when we moved here.

Some of the varieties, we can't find here anymore. But there are others that we found here. For example, our favorite is kasindol, which has red skin and yellow flesh that tastes very sweet. Hence, it is very easy to sell in the market. We also plant *bilaka*, which is very powdery; *klarin*, which is sweet with elongated roots that do not cluster in one area (hence difficult for us to harvest); *inanahaw*, which has red skin, yellow flesh, and produces many roots; *katimpa*, which has big sweet-tasting roots with yellow skin and flesh and fingerlike leaves; *katuka*, which has rounded leaves and roots, powdery in texture and bland in taste; *kalugti*, which has small, rounded leaves and elongated roots, the flesh of which is so powdery and dry that the skin cracks when being cooked; and *manabang*, another powdery variety with various sizes and shapes of roots.

There are many uses for sweet potatoes; all parts can in fact be used. The leaves, especially the tops, are good as vegetables. For salad we just blanch them and put some spices and vinegar. It is very appetizing. Boiled and filtered with a net bag and then mixed with *kalamansi* [local lemon] and some sugar, the leaves make nutritious "*camote* juice." Leaves can also be used as medicine to heal skin diseases. For this purpose, one has to broil sweet potato leaves wrapped in banana leaves and then rub these over the affected area. Healing proceeds very rapidly. As for the roots, we make snacks— sweetened, boiled, fried, or mashed—and also use these as a staple food during lean times. We also feed sweet potato leaves and roots to our pigs.

I like to plant different varieties of sweet potatoes so we can choose from different tastes and textures. The bland varieties are good to eat with dried fish when we run out of corn or rice. When they are bland and dry, they are also delicious with meat and soup. Bland, watery ones go well with coffee. Dry and sweet varieties are preferred by children for snacks and can be served with water only since they are satisfying by themselves. But I personally don't like to eat the sweet kinds because I get satiated quickly and choke very easily.

Like I said before, we had been planting sweet potatoes since we were in Leyte, so when we moved here we followed almost the same ways from land preparation to harvesting. The former can be done with grab hoe and other metal implements, but the latter is always done with wooden or bamboo sticks so we do not damage the young roots. Planting is done during low tide so the roots will be big and stay near the surface of the soil instead of going down (which will make it difficult to harvest). Since we are now far from the sea, we cannot see the tide, but we know it is low tide when the moon is new or when the pupils of the eyes of the cat are small. This was taught to us by our elders. Of course, now we can also refer to a calendar for the lunar cycle.

In planting, we always loosen the soil first and make little hills, then plant three cuttings per hill. In covering the cuttings with soil, we spread our hands on top of the soil so that there will be as many roots as we have fingers. If there are pests, we do not control them with chemicals. We just let them eat what they can; after all, they cannot consume all of it. In any case, weevils attack only during the dry season, not during the wet. You see, pest attacks are also seasonal. In Leyte, we never used fertilizers, either, but here in Salvacion people use fertilizers. It has become a habit, so that plants have learned to depend on its application and will not grow "beautifully" unless fertilized. I have observed the weevil problem also worsens when fertilizer is used.

We have no problem with storage since we don't harvest all roots at once. We get only the big ones first and return all the small ones and cover them with soil so they have more time to grow. The first harvest must be broiled and rubbed with ashes so that the sweet potatoes left in the field will not be attacked by weevil and the flesh will become powdery in texture. If we harvest a lot and feel like keeping some or waiting for them to ripen, we do not wash the roots that we will not eat yet, so they will not rot. We dig a small pit, line it with leaves and grasses, and place the roots there. Then we cover them with leaves and grasses and a sack and, finally, with a layer of soil. The roots can last for a month this way.

I am seventy-four now, and we are still planting several kinds of sweet potatoes. I am interested in planting as many different kinds as I can get cuttings of. Now, also, when my children come asking for rice, we harvest sweet potatoes, sell them in the market, and get cash to buy rice.

WOMEN, MICROENVIRONMENTS, AND GENETIC CONSERVATION

What is the special place of women in sustaining diversity in the face of modernization? Aside from the Lamarckian truism that to keep something in use is to keep it from disappearing—and women are the main utilizers of food crop germplasm—women also possess detailed agricultural knowledge and intimate knowledge of plants. Because in most cultures the day-to-day subsistence of the household rests principally on the women's shoulders, there is great pressure on women to pay attention to farming and botanical information in order for their families to survive.

Also revealing are the local evaluation criteria elicited using the triads test as summarized in table 3.3. Looking at the sums by informant category, it can be seen that, overall, more descriptions or criteria are known to and employed by females than males. It is also interesting to note that there is less discrepancy between males and females in Intavas, where sweet potato production is still nearly at a subsistence level (and male and female labor is not sharply segregated), than in Salvacion, where commercialization of production is in a more advanced state (and sexual division of labor is more sharply delineated).

Focusing on specific subtotals by informant category for each group of local criteria, it can be seen that in both Intavas and Salvacion females are more conversant than males with respect to morphological, gastronomic, and functional criteria. The criteria utilized more by males than by females are limited to life habits and agronomic criteria in Intavas, and familiarity of variety in Salvacion. The former are of course more related to direct cultivation requirements, while the latter has greater bearing on the management of resources with respect to the procurement of planting materials and input, as well as marketing of output. In keeping with what is expected to happen in cash cropping, males are better versed than females in Salvacion with respect to varietal familiarity and, indirectly, marketability of crops. As a point of

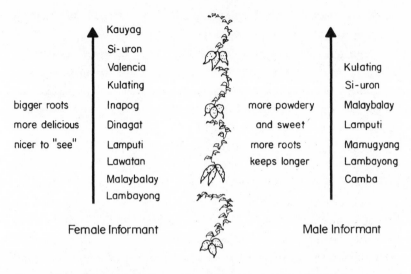

bigger roots	Kauyag			Kulating
more delicious	Si-uron			Si-uron
nicer to "see"	Valencia		more powdery	Malaybalay
	Kulating		and sweet	Lamputi
	Inapog		more roots	Mamugyang
	Dinagat		keeps longer	Lambayong
	Lamputi			Camba
	Lawatan			
	Malaybalay			
	Lambayong			

Female Informant   Male Informant

Figure 5.1. Indigenous criteria used in ranking sweet potato varieties.

comparison, the indigenous criteria used in ranking sweet potato varieties by a female and a male informant are presented in figure 5.1.

Research on the role of women in relation to other crops bears out the above conclusions pertaining to women's intimate knowledge of, and empathy with, the conservation of diversity. According to Janice Jiggins, Kpelle women rice growers recognize at least one hundred varieties of rice and use a systematic framework for describing rice, relying on attributes such as "husk and seed color, length of hair at the tip of the rice, size of the grain, ease with which husk can be removed, length of time required to cook, and suitability to different types of soil and terrain" (1986:18). In my work among rice farmers in rural Philippines, I found that women in general understand the intricacies of the production and marketing of rice, vegetables, and ornamental plants and utilize more criteria than men, ranging from agronomic to gastronomic, in recognizing and categorizing crop varieties (Nazarea-Sandoval 1995). Women have traditionally selected seeds based on many different parameters, such as multiple uses, cross-crop interactions, stability, and maturation periods (Lipton 1989). In the case of bean selection in Rwanda—and, one suspects, in other cases as well—women are the "experts," although their husbands determine their participation in field trials (Sperling 1992: 101). James Boster, in studying Aguaruna manioc inventories, noted that cuttings of manioc are actively exchanged through a network of kinswomen, with the emphasis being on keeping "a good mix" of cultivars when planting new gardens (1984:35).

Women as direct users of food crop germplasm, women as decision makers in the maintenance of different traditional varieties and indigenous technologies, women as repositories of detailed agricultural knowledge, and women as socializing agents in cultural transmission all add up to women as significant actual and potential partners in the conservation of the diversity of important crops. As Vandana Shiva noted, "The logic of diversity is best derived from biodiversity and women's links to it. It helps to look at dominant structures from below, from the grounds of diversity, which reveal monocultures to be unproductive and the knowledge that produces them as primitive rather than sophisticated" (1993:165). Women like Elena Gayunan and Concordia Gerong are by no means exceptional leaders in their respective communities. They are typical women (to the extent that this is possible) who can be found in almost any farming community and for whom genetic conservation may be taken for granted as a way of life.

The nurturance of diversity at the margins, be it due to fuzziness of decision-making criteria or a certain degree of independence from the cash economy (or a combination of both), offers, I think, an optimistic prognosis on the resistance of agricultural knowledge systems and practices. This is parallel to Robert Chambers's assertion that "in both agricultural and social sciences . . . complexity and diversity are underperceived, and therefore undervalued" (1990b:3). Chambers goes on to discuss "biases in perception"—such as the choice of convenient sites for experimentation, field visits governed by an ethos of rural development tourism, and a lack of curiosity beyond narrow physical and disciplinary domains—that make us insensitive to farmers' experiments and informal networks, their cognition of varieties and technologies, and their long-term survival strategies. In other words, we need to take heed of what goes on in more sheltered, small-scale "microenvironments" in order to appreciate farmers' positive contributions to diversity.

Two caveats need to be taken into consideration, however, before optimism lulls us into complacency. One is that there are, in reality, economic, technological, and political forces that threaten diversity, and even microenvironments at the fringes are not completely insulated. Nor are pockets of memories totally resistant. There is a need to strengthen institutional and cultural responsiveness (even vigilance) to conscious evaluation—and, when the situation warrants, modification or rejection—of development options that are presented. Second, not many social or agricultural scientists have the luxury of conducting long-term studies or surveying every aberrant case, however interesting or delightful. However, the local people that we work with have had this "luxury" imposed upon them by the necessity of living their lives in these microenvironments. They possess the curiosity, the knowledge, and the memories about agricultural alternatives that worked in the past and could work—with some fine-tuning, updating, and dovetailing—well into the future.

6

CULTURAL ALTERNATIVES IN IN SITU GERMPLASM CONSERVATION

By the end of Phase I of the memory banking project, roughly one and a half years after its inception, we had collected and preserved herbarium specimens of eighty-nine traditional sweet potato varieties in Bukidnon, Philippines. Attached to each voucher specimen was a collection data sheet that included the standard passport data, supplemented by information on uses and local evaluations. A local germplasm collection of landraces from different ethnic groups in Bukidnon had been established and replicated at the International Potato Center (CIP) station in Malaybalay, Bukidnon (see fig. 3.1). The planting material for this collection was brought to the station by representatives of different ethnic groups in Bukidnon who planted the cuttings according to their traditional ways. Subsequently, planting materials from these original cuttings were propagated in adjacent plots under the supervision of a sweet potato plant breeder and curator. The local germplasm collection in Malaybalay is a ready source of planting materials for farmers around the area, and festivities are organized periodically to make more people aware of its existence. Samples of this collection have been given to, and are being propagated by, the Institute of Plant Breeding (IPB) at the University of the Philippines at Los Baños (UPLB), the Tarlac Agricultural College (TAC) in Camiling, Tarlac, and the CIP Station in Batac, Ilocos Sur. Evaluation of the agronomic performance and weevil resistance of these varieties has been undertaken at the different sites.

The second phase of the memory banking project, consisting of cultural experiments in in situ germplasm conservation, was intended to take the memory banking initiative one step further in two parallel and complementary directions: (1) transferring the main responsibility for documenting indigenous agricultural knowledge from researchers to farmer-custodians, and (2) moving the germplasm collection even closer to the source by forging a partnership between scientists and users in the establishment and maintenance of in situ germplasm collections. Another objective was to document and compare two novel approaches to in situ gene banking. One was through a male political hierarchy based on traditional notions of power and control; the other was through an informal network of migrant women based on a more or less egalitarian camaraderie. Our criteria for choosing groups to work with were shaped by our observations about the greater persistence of cultural and genetic diversity along the margins of commercial production systems among subsistence-oriented farmers and women, as discussed in the previous chapter.

In situ gene banking is the conservation of plant genetic resources in locations where they normally thrive, or the maintenance of diversity in their natural environment, such as in traditional agro-ecosystems for landraces (Altieri and Merrick 1987; Oldfield and Alcorn 1991). From our experience, it was a natural offshoot of memory banking, because once people got started thinking more intensively and collectively about varieties valued and varieties lost, they started wondering where some of the traditional varieties had gone and questioning the necessity and inevitability of their loss. Laments like these, for example, were commonly expressed:

> We plant these varieties now because they are the only ones available. If there were other traditional varieties, we would plant them too, for they are more delicious than the new ones.

> Some of the old varieties just disappeared because people wanted different crops or different varieties. As a result, some which were neglected slowly vanished. Now, we no longer have them.

These farmers are not, as we tend to portray them, just passive "victims" of agricultural development who need to be enlightened or "empowered." Whether their motivation is to reserve some production for household consumption or to alternately maximize and hedge against market demand and agronomic performance, farmers often nurture diversity consciously and actively in their home gardens and their fields, as these comments reveal:

Most of my land is used for planting the variety that can be easily sold in the market. This is the sweet and powdery kind. But on the margins, as you can see, I cultivate different kinds, as many as I can get cuttings of. Those varieties that are sweet but won't sell in the market because they are watery are for our snacks. The bland and dry ones we use as substitutes for rice and bread. The bland but watery ones we feed to our pigs.

We plant five kinds at any one time to test from which ones we get the most benefit. During different seasons, one should have different kinds because one cannot tell which ones will yield the most or sell at the best price in the market. So we plant five different varieties each time. We ask for planting materials from our neighbors, but we don't mix them up.

According to John Holden, James Peacock, and Trevor Williams, "the pressures of agricultural and industrial development in the past hundred years have been so powerful and the consequent changes so rapid, that the only effective response to crisis has been to collect and conserve—usually seeds in cold storage— representative samples of crop diversity" (1993:9). Operating under the mandate of the Consultive Group for International Agricultural Research (CGIAR), several International Agricultural Research Centers are charged with the collection, management, and distribution of plant genetic resources in the form of seeds, living plants, and in vitro tissue cultures (FAO 1989; Hawkes 1991). National research systems replicate these agenda on a smaller scale. Ex situ conservation protects plant genetic resources from loss due to natural, social, and political instabilities and neglect (Van Soest 1990; Rhoades 1991; Huaman and Schneidiche 1991) but are subject to sampling oversights and loss due to genetic drift and germplasm degeneration. In addition, the holdings of gene banks are largely insulated from evolutionary forces that could give rise to better-adapted genotypes (Wilkes 1984; Anikster 1988; Zimmerman and Douches 1991).

By comparison, in situ gene banking has the potential for melding preservation with adaptation in communities where the plants have traditionally been grown. Moreover, compared to other forms of in situ conservation— such as biosphere reserves and botanical gardens that do a good job of conserving biodiversity in the wild or well-tended state (Ingram 1990; Heywood 1990) but operate, for the most part, on the principle of exclusion of indigenous groups—in situ gene banking of crop genetic resources involves farmers from the outset and builds upon local resources and practices. As such, it promotes greater access to, and sovereignty over, crops that are in existence mainly because of farmers' activities over centuries of breeding, selection, and cultivation.

In situ germplasm conservation of agricultural crops places both the power over and the responsibility for plant genetic resources squarely in the farmers' hands. At the same time, the present generation of farmers can serve as custodians of indigenous knowledge and can be strongly motivated to transmit this knowledge to the next generation. Yet while it is easy enough to justify the preservation of genetic diversity in situ, and while well-argued works on the subject matter can be found in the literature (Nabhan 1986; Altieri and Merrick 1987; Soleri and Cleveland 1993), the messy part comes with the actual operationalization and translation of paper concepts to diverse fields. Problems of incentives, long-term maintenance, farmer subsidies, intellectual property rights to both the varieties and the associated knowledge, and proprietary right and access to collections then come into play.

There are definite advantages—as well as difficulties— attendant on every technique of plant genetic conservation. In situ gene banking is no exception. For all the merits just discussed, it has the drawbacks of being complicated to implement and subject to loss due to natural calamities, sociopolitical flux, and lack of sustained interest and responsibility (Brush 1991; Hawkes 1991). Therefore, the only logical and tenable recourse is complementation between established ex situ conservation efforts and in situ initiatives. For this complementation to occur, farmers' long-term conservation practices as demonstrated in the microenvironments that they nurture (i.e., their home gardens and their polycultures [Alcorn 1984; Cleveland and Soleri 1987; Paddock and de Jong 1991]) must be understood in the context of their knowledge, technologies, criteria, and constraints (both direct and indirect). Only then can we hope to enhance local-level biodiversity conservation and link this in a mutually beneficial manner to national, regional, and global initiatives. This is what we set out to do in Bukidnon during Phase II of the memory banking project—with varying and surprising degrees of success.

After visiting several possible sites in Bukidnon and talking with the local population to explore the possibility of establishing an in situ gene bank for traditional root crops, two sites—Dalwangan in Malaybalay and Maambong in Libona—were selected (figs. 6.1 and 6.5). In choosing the sites, the foremost considerations were the possibility of comparing results in several dimensions and the prospect of sustaining the project initiative at the local level. Several sites in Bukidnon were considered but eliminated due to inaccessibility, unstable peace and order conditions, and/or lack of interest among community members.

In Dalwangan, the population is predominantly composed of native Bukidnons who cultivate three major cash crops—corn, coffee, and abaca. Production of root crops is less commercialized than in Maambong, and the local farmers still reserve much of their produce for subsistence. By contrast, Maambong is populated by Visayan migrants from Bohol and Cebu, and many farmers are engaged in a moderately commercialized production of sweet potatoes in addition to corn, which is the major cash crop.

Initial contact in Dalwangan was made through the local chieftain, or *datu*, and subsequent meetings were held with representatives from the council of elders, the farmers' organization, and the youth organization. The majority of these initial contacts were male. In Maambong, additional contacts were made with the help of the female key informants of the memory banking project and the *baranggay* captain.[1] The group expanded to include their friends, relatives and ceremonial kin, and members of the local mothers' club. In both sites, we discussed the rationale and objectives of the project and together with the interested parties threshed out the details of implementation. We emphasized that the project was envisioned to be a true and equal partnership between scientists and farmers in the preservation of the diversity of locally valued root crops, so the arrangements should be mutually satisfactory and sustainable in the long run. Questions about incentives, access, monitoring, responsibilities, and rewards were also openly explored in a series of visits and community meetings. In the following sections, I discuss in greater detail the in situ germplasm conservation projects that we initiated in the two areas, compare the trajectories taken by the two projects, and discuss the implications for in situ conservation of plant genetic resources.

KAUYAGAN SA KAHILAWAN: AN INCOME-GENERATING PROJECT IN DALWANGAN

The name of this project component was derived from a native Binukid term meaning "livelihood for the people." The name was coined by the local leadership to signify the incorporation of income-generating activities, such as

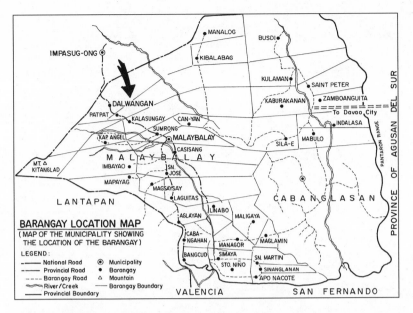

Figure 6.1. Location map of Dalwangan, Malaybalay (source: *Barangay Profile & 5-Year Development Plan, 1985–1989*).

goat, chicken, and swine raising, into the maintenance of indigenous land-races of root crops. This project component was based in Dalwangan, Malay-balay (fig. 6.1), and was organized and managed in collaboration with the local political leadership composed of datus, the council of elders, and orga-nized youth.

The project area that we started with consisted of 3,999 square meters of land donated by a member of the leading datu's extended family. Located along the riverbank of the Sawaga River, the project area included part of the river and its surrounding land (fig. 6.2). The section closest to the river was designated as a natural reserve or sanctuary for wild relatives of root crops. The cleared area near the riverbank was allocated for the cultivation of farm-ers' landraces of root crops such as yam, taro, and sweet potatoes. The rest of the area was cleared by the youth in anticipation of developing it for livestock raising. It was envisioned that in this way the youth would be profitably oc-cupied while taking care of the in situ germplasm collection. Excess roots, tubers, and leaves from the cultivated area were to be used to feed the animals raised by the local collaborators.

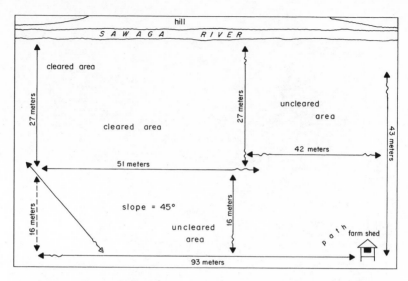

Figure 6.2. Dalwangan, Malaybalay, in situ germplasm collection and maintenance site.

Management of the collection in Dalwangan, Malaybalay, was in the
hands of the local political hierarchy. The existing relationships and organizational structure among the principal actors involved are depicted in figures
6.3 and 6.4, respectively. Note that all the participants were male, connected
to each other by membership in the tribal council, farmers' organization, and
youth organization, as well as through kinship. In addition to fostering the
gene banking and livelihood activities, one of the objectives of this project
was to strengthen the mechanism of transmission of traditional agricultural
knowledge from the elderly to the young. One mode of transmission that we
wanted to explore was through political and kinship linkages, as depicted in
figure 6.3.

Table 6.1 summarizes the variety of root crops existing in Dalwangan at
the inception of the project as revealed by a cursory baseline survey. The local
population values traditional varieties of root crops as sources of food, medicine, and fodder. Because the Dalwagan population is predominantly composed of native Bukidnons, the traditional value of root crops as famine food
is still widely recognized.

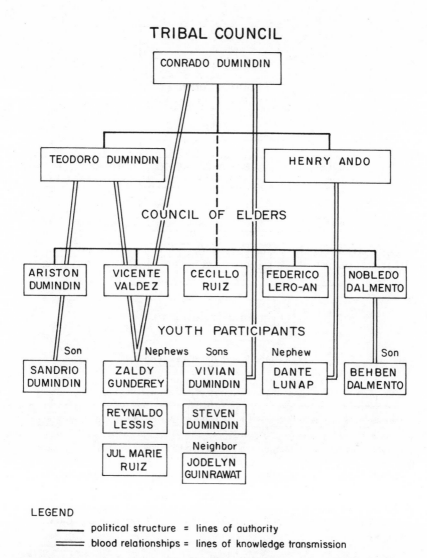

Figure 6.3. Existing relationships among interested parties in Dalwangan, Malaybalay.

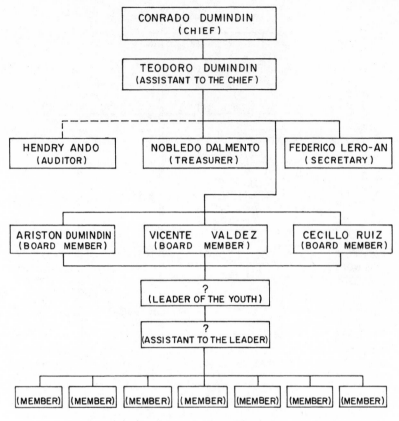

Note: The leaders of the youth will be chosen jointly by the elders and the youth

Figure 6.4. Proposed organizational structure of Kauyagan sa Kahilawan.

TABLE 6.1. Baseline Root Crop Diversity in Dalwangan, Malaybalay, in 1992

Common Name	Varieties Observed and/or Reported
Sweet potato (*camote*)	10 varieties, approximately
Cassava (*binggala*)	2 varieties, viz. *kulikot* (white) and *uropa* (yellow)
Taro (*gabi*)	8 varieties, viz. *tiyali, bagikay, lumalag, buol uwak, luman-tod, binaliti, balikuod, bagyang*
Wild relatives	*lab-o* (wild yam), *apusaw* (wild taro), *tandug, payaw* (pain reliever), *biga* (edible root)

INAHAN NGA MAKUGIHON: THE INFORMAL NETWORK OF MIGRANT WOMEN IN MAAMBONG

The name of this project component was derived from a Visayan term meaning "industrious mothers." The name was coined by migrant women in Maambong, Libona, to denote the involvement of mothers in the preservation of traditional varieties of root crops in the area through continuous cultivation and use. The project was managed by the women of Maambong (where the in situ collection was based) and Salvacion (the sitio that was one of the sites of the memory banking project), who expressed an interest in further collaboration with us.

The project was situated in an 840 square meter piece of idle land that was donated by Lydia *vda. de* Casseres, an elderly woman, so she would "be remembered after [her] death." The location of Maambong and Salvacion (fig. 6.5) and the degree of commercialization of crop production, as well as the intensity of land use in the area, have led to and necessitated a different kind of spatial arrangement for the in situ gene banking project. Compared to Dalwangan, the project in Maambong was located on a significantly smaller piece of idle land adjacent to other parcels of cultivated land owned by the donor (fig. 6.6). In contrast to Dalwangan, there was no area designated as a reserve or sanctuary since, as the women themselves observed, most parcels of land had been under commercial and semicommercial cultivation for some time, and many varieties of root crops "vanished," especially when the farmers in the area leased or sold their land to Del Monte, which converted these tracts of land to pineapple plantations.

The style of management was different, too, because the women were informally linked through bonds of friendship, kinship, business ventures, religious affiliations, and membership in a loosely structured village organization called the Mother's Craft (fig. 6.7). The essentially egalitarian structure was maintained in the management of the in situ collection (fig. 6.8). In lieu of a reserve, the women worked through their informal networks to enrich the existing varietal diversity — or pursue germplasm enhancement — by asking for planting materials from market associates, friends from neighboring sitios, and relatives from their hometowns.

The women maintained the collections in individual rows, like home gardens, and operated them on the principle of conservation through use.

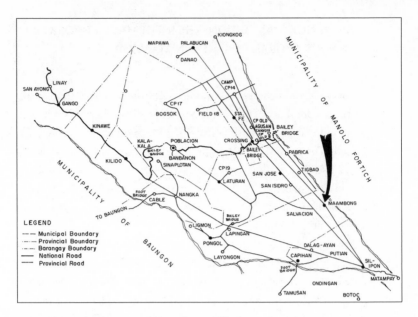

Figure 6.5. Location map of Maambong, Libona.

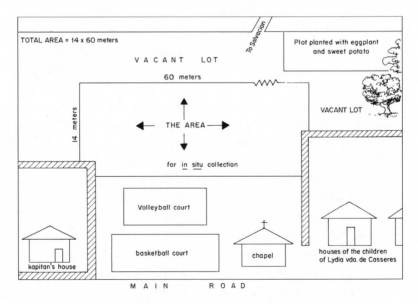

Figure 6.6. Maambong, Libona, in situ germplasm collection and maintenance site.

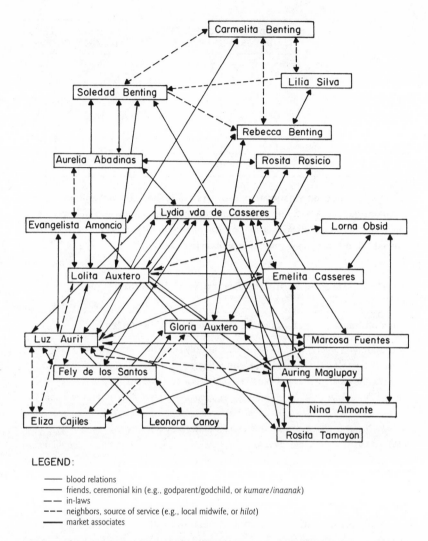

LEGEND:

——— blood relations
——— friends, ceremonial kin (e.g., godparent/godchild, or *kumare/inaanak*)
— — in-laws
- - - neighbors, source of service (e.g., local midwife, or *hilot*)
——— market associates

Figure 6.7. Existing networks among interested parties in Maambong, Libona.

Aside from their seemingly inherent empathy with the idea of genetic conservation, the women were motivated by camaraderie and opportunities for field visits, as well as by the prospect of participating in a contest as to whose root crop garden was the most diverse after a period of time had elapsed. Finally, there was the additional incentive of getting a share in the harvest. They agreed among themselves and with the donor of the land that 5 percent of the harvest would go to the donor, while the rest would be kept or sold by each participant.

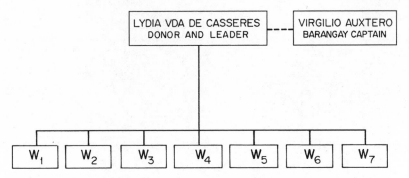

Figure 6.8. Proposed organizational structure of Inahan nga Makugihon. The barangay captain will be responsible for land preparation and will oversee the project as an ex officio member of the management organization. The boxes labeled W$_N$ indicate the women who will be involved.

TABLE 6.2. Baseline Root Crop Diversity in Maambong, Libona, in 1992

Common Name	Varieties Observed and/or Reported
Sweet potato (*camote*)	4 varieties commonly cultivated, viz. *kasindol, klarin, Sil-ipon*, and *5-finger*
Cassava (*binggala*)	2 varieties, viz. *miracle* (yellow) and *Negros* (white)
Taro (*gabi*)	3 varieties, viz. *ginabe* (violet), *kinisol* (white) and *gabi tsina* (white)
Tarolike (*lutia*)	2 varieties, viz. *kinisol* and *lumalayog*
Wild relatives	*paa sa dalaga* (wild taro), *salayaw* (red taro), *lima-lima* (turniplike root crop), and *balot* (tarolike root crop)

Table 6.2 presents the baseline varietal diversity in Maambong. One interesting aspect of this project component is that it was based in a moderately commercialized—and therefore impoverished—area in terms of genetic diversity of root crops. Yet it was organized and managed by migrant women who had preserved a recollection of diversity *in their minds*. The in situ germplasm conservation project thus served the women of Maambong as an opportunity to translate "memories" into home garden realities.

A series of dialogues was conducted with those interested in participating in Dalwangan and Maambong to chart the mechanisms of collaboration and to settle the details of implementation. The local participants planned out their activities for the first year, and these time frames are presented in figure 6.9.

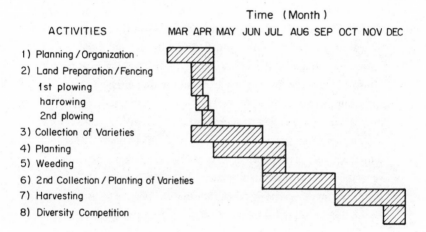

Figure 6.9 Proposed timetables for Kauyagan sa Kahilawan (top) and Inahan nga Makugihon (bottom).

DIFFERENT STYLES, DIFFERENT TRAJECTORIES

As previously stated, we were guided in our choice of groups to work with by our earlier finding that diversity, as well as affinity thereto, flourishes at the margins. Thus, we sought out as partners the native subsistence farmers of Dalwangan and the women growers and traders of Maambong. Aside from considerations of the likelihood of interest, the choice was also prompted by the potential for comparison, i.e., a male-dominated political structure compared to an egalitarian and informal female network. Needless to say, organizational structure and gender were aspects that we thought were worth paying attention to from the outset.

A more textured background in personalties and dynamics might contribute a better appreciation of the results. Toward this end, I include a condensed life history of Lydia *vda. de* Casseres, the donor of the land for the in situ germplasm collection in Maambong, followed by excerpts from the meeting we had with the prospective collaborators from Dalwangan. Note that the life history was elicited as part of the memory banking project. The meeting involved farmers in Dalwangan who were mostly village leaders and in that capacity had previously attended many government-sponsored meetings in and outside Bukidnon.

My name is Lydia *vda. de* Casseres. I am sixty-two years old. I was born in Tabuan, Bohol. I grew up and received primary education in that area, but only up to fourth grade. I have not experienced becoming a maid or helper in any house or sleeping in different houses. This is because my mother told me that girls who were always going outside would be attacked by *bangkaw* [monster]. It was only when I got married that I moved, because my husband's work took us here. We settled and grew old here in Salvacion. We maintained a piggery and planted sweet potato, rice, corn, and different vegetables. We also planted banana and many other crops to augment our income. The sweet potato that we planted in Bohol was *klarin* only. It has red skin and white flesh. It is also quite delicious.

Here, we used to have 5-finger, *valencia*, *sil-ipon*, which has white flesh and skin but is not sweet, and *kinampay*, which has violet skin and flesh. The variety which occupies the largest portion of our land here is 5-finger, which is also called *kasindol*. Other varieties have disappeared, and my children are tired of looking for them. Those which disappeared are kinampay, sil-ipon, *initlog*, which is like an egg, and klarin. Maybe there are still some of these varieties in the most remote farms. These varieties disappeared because they were not cultivated anymore. Maybe if my husband were still alive today he would continue to cultivate the traditional varieties. He got the kinampay variety from Lunukan, Manolo Fortich, Bukidnon. But he died ten years ago, hence all is gone now. The new variety is kasindol, or 5-finger, and I have no idea where this came from. This variety is also being planted by my children.

Planting is done during low tide. My guide in determining if it is low tide is the cat, because this is what my parents have taught me. I do not know if you are going to believe me. This is done by looking at the eyeball [pupil] of the cat. If it is small, then it is low tide; if it is big, then it is high tide. But most of the time it is during November that we do the planting. This is because the sweet potato root is expensive during the month of March and April, so if you plant this in the month of November, then you will be ready to harvest by March or April.

Whenever I plant, I always use holy water, a snail, and the fruit of a certain wood called *tubog*. We include tubog with the planting materials for the roots to be many, and the snail is for the roots to cluster in one area. Holy water is also included for God to take care of my crop.

Before, it was my husband who did the planting, but now that he is dead, I am the one doing it. It was my husband who did it in the past because I did the household chores. He collected the three things that I have mentioned, so by the time that he went home, it was already noon. The next morning, he would plant many vines. But now I do it all alone.

We are using *purok* (a long knife) in planting. But we also practice the slash-and-burn method. This will be followed by plowing using carabao. After the area is cleared, the crop will be planted. We used to hire laborers for about ₱15.00/day/person. But we only had two laborers. We got the payment for them by selling our chickens.

Regarding rats, I walk around the area and say something like "Rats, please do not eat all my plants, for I also eat them, because, as you know, I am only poor." This is done while walking around the area. There is an owner or god of rats also, so you should give them respect.

In harvesting, we use a wooden stick so that the vines and roots will not be damaged, especially those which are still small. If you use wood, you can determine which ones are big and which ones are small. Moreover, before actually harvesting, we offer eggs for the roots to be powdery and sugarcane for it to be sweet. I offer them to God with my thanksgiving prayer so that he will take care of my sweet potato roots. We do not store the roots. After harvesting we eat or sell them, unlike corn, which we store.

Among the varieties which I have mentioned, I like klarin best because it produces many roots. Even the climbing vines will bear some roots. But generally I like all of them. I eat only one at a time, or two at most, because I easily get choked when I eat too much. If there are more roots than can be eaten, we sell them in the market on Sunday. Roots that we cannot sell will be fed to pigs. More and more, I plant just for myself and for my pigs. We use our harvest to prepare fried sweet potato, *kidkiron* [porridge], and *suman* [steamed rolls], and the leaves can be used as vegetables. Sweet potato can also be used as medicine for itchy skin. The roots will be shredded and placed on the affected area.

Aside from sweet potato, we also cultivate other crops like cassava, taro, and vegetables. We also plant corn for home consumption. What we like about sweet potato is that it is easy to sell. Every Sunday when we go to market, it will be weighed and, presto, it is sold! We also buy some other things that are needed at home. This crop helped us in renovating our house. I was also able to buy clothes and an armoire from the income from sweet potato.

Below are excerpts from a February 29, 1992, meeting with the datu, other members of the local leadership, and youth representatives in Dalwangan, Bukidnon:

A. On root crops and in situ conservation:

Question: Is there a native term for root crops? Can you please tell us what it is.

Response 1: *Amulan.*

Response 2: That is just one kind. They are asking us what we call all root crops taken together.

Response 3: *Lagutmon.*

Response 4: But that is a Visayan term. They want a Binukid [native] term.

Response 5: *Tigkauhol*, now that's a native term.

Response 6: Let's think a bit more about it. Until now I'm not quite sure what the native term is for root crops. Maybe it's *kauyagan*, because *kauyagan* for us means anything that's edible. It does not include all plants, only those that can be eaten.

Response 7: Better call it *kauyagan sa bugto* to specify that root crops grow underground.

Question: Where would be the best place to establish a root crop collection? Can we find such a place around here?

Response 1: Near the river we can find several root crops growing wild.

Response 2: Yes, near the Sawaga River there is *payaw, lab-o, apusaw.*

Response 3: The area can be reached. It is about two to three kilometers down the road. There we can find apusaw, *bag-yang*, lab-o, and *tandog-tandog*. There are some snakes, though.

Question: Do you know who owns the land?

Response: My older brother.

Question: Do you think we can use his property for our project? They might decide later that we cannot use it. It would be a waste of effort.

Response: Maybe we can draw a memorandum of agreement.

   B. On the purpose and philosophy behind in situ gene banking:

Datu: We need a project like this for the elderly to be involved in. They will be the source of wisdom. The youth will learn from them and maintain the collection.

Researcher: Yes, precisely. How do you see it operating?

Datu: The elderly farmers will be "the brains." We have to transfer what they know to our youth. We must explain to our youth what we are doing so that it will have some meaning for them. By the way, will the elderly receive some kind of "honorarium" for the training they will give?

   C. On community participation and compensation:

Researcher: The next question is, How do we go about establishing the collection? Who will maintain it? We need to talk about these matters so we can sustain this initiative, keep it going.

Datu: It's like this. When the youth have a project involving maintenance of the root crops, they should have a livelihood project in addition. They have to get something for the attention they give to the collection and for their time. We have to add another project component such as livestock raising—for example, goats, chickens, and pigs—to make it worth their while.

Researcher: You don't think the goats would cross over to the gardens and eat the root crops?

Datu: Oh, no. We will build a fence around the livestock. We will feed the goats and chickens with excess vines, leaves, and root crops. And then we can even use the droppings as fertilizer. In this way, we can approximate the true situation of the farmer with root crops and livestock both—you know, diversified.

TRANSFORMATIONS AND OUTCOMES

After the stage was set for the in situ gene banking initiatives in Dalwangan and Maambong, I unfortunately had to leave UPWARD and the Philippines for another job. I say "unfortunately" only in the sense that I would have liked very much to see the project through and witness the "roots" of our labor. A more positive way of looking at it, however, is that because I was no longer there to influence the project, there was no way I could bias the results to reflect the hypotheses I was testing, particularly those about gender and informal structures in relation to in situ gene banking. Moreover, the project was taken over by a male social scientist, Gordon Prain, the coordinator of UPWARD.[2] Any potential gender affinity (and/or polarity) between the researcher and local farmers that could swing the results one way or the other was therefore considerably reduced or balanced out.

The anticipated organizational structure among the principal actors in Dalwangan (see fig. 6.4) did not hold for very long. Instead, because the land for the in situ germplasm collection was donated by the datu's brother, his extended family more or less took over the gene banking initiatives from planting onward. In fact, even during the preparatory activities, people either slipped away at various times during the day or just stayed out of "shame" (Prain and Piniero 1994).

Eventually, the maintenance of the Dalwangan root crop gene bank became the day-to-day responsibility of the female kin of the datu's brother's

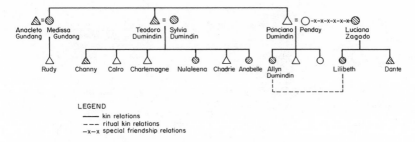

LEGEND
——— kin relations
– – – ritual kin relations
–x–x special friendship relations

Figure 6.10. Relationships in the de facto curator group of the Dalwangan gene bank (from Prain and Piniero 1994).

household, with male participation mostly confined to land preparation (fig. 6.10). When the long dry season decimated the germplasm collection, one of the women "rescued" a third of the varieties and established her own "gene bank" in the form of a home garden. Other women followed suit, planting cuttings of different varieties in their own home gardens. These cuttings came from the Dalwangan in situ collection, the nearby International Potato Center (CIP) local gene bank that we had earlier established with various ethnic groups in Bukidnon, and the Maambong in situ collection. Essentially, therefore, what started as a male authority–enforced group curatorship disintegrated in favor of a patchwork of multiple-curatorship, home garden–style collections established and maintained by the women linked through kinship, natural relations, and friendship bonds.

In Maambong, the local gene banking effort was pursued with a light-hearted communal spirit from the planning up to the maintenance of the collection. Men and children joined in the land preparation and planting, both of which were completed in one day. Interest was sustained by the camaraderie that prevailed among the women curators. The informal network that they started with, with the migrant women constituting the Inahan nga Makugihan (fig. 6.7), became more and more complex, with multiple links established among gene bank collaborators (fig. 6.11). Lydia *vda. de* Casseres, the donor of the land, became a moral rather than a political/organizational leader, encouraging participation mainly by example and by enjoining neighbors, friends, and kin to fulfill their responsibilities.

We anticipated that the root crop germplasm collection in Maambong would grow by flow and accretion of germplasm through different "pathways," such as blood relations, ceremonial kinship, and exchange between market associates. As it turned out, the main source of germplasm enhance-

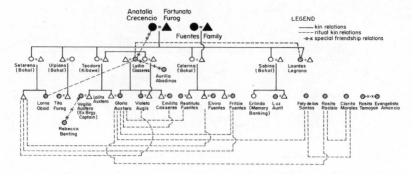

Figure 6.11. Relationships in the de facto curator group of the Maambong gene bank (from Prain and Piniero 1994).

ment was exchange between neighbors. Thus, any variety that was obtained by one participant was shared until it spread among all or almost all of them (Prain and Piniero 1994). The resulting redundancy constituted a natural backup system in case of loss of cultivars in any of the rows of the in situ gene bank. It also demonstrated that there was a well-entrenched cultural ethic of sharing coupled with an active interest in soliciting when it came to plant genetic resources, at least in terms of food crops. Finally, it showed that communal in situ gene banks did not compete with home gardens but rather that the two forms of local germplasm conservation could actually enrich and reinforce each other.

For purposes of comparison, the current "outcomes" in terms of relationships of the major players in in situ gene banking in Dalwangan's Kauyagan sa Kahilawan project and Maambong's Inahan nga Makugihon project are reproduced from Prain and Piniero's paper (1994:204, 208) in figures 6.10 and 6.11. Surprisingly, although root crop diversity in the Dalwangan project site may be significantly less than that in the Maambong project site, the "rescued" genetic resources are alive and spreading informally among the women's home gardens. This is one indicator of diversity—perhaps we can call it fugitive diversity—that was not measured by Prain and Piniero. Thus, from the more specific research objective of testing alternative arrangements in in situ gene banking, the male-dominated political structure failed. However, from the point of view of the larger, and more important, goal of germplasm conservation and enhancement, the Dalwangan case was an unexpected success, with many lessons to teach. In a paradoxical way, it was reminiscent of the anecdote about the agricultural extension agent who introduced a high-yielding variety of corn to a traditional, risk-averse community by fencing off the experimental plot and thus enticing farmers to pilfer "valuable" seeds for planting in their own fields. By comparison, the increase in diversity in Maambong, a commercialized area in terms of sweet potato production and an area that was practically stripped of its wild root crop population because of the conversion of large tracts of land to pineapple plantations, attested to the resilience of agricultural systems and farmers in relation to genetic erosion and conservation.

Our experience in Bukidnon supports the arguments by Altieri and Merrick (1987) and Brush (1991) on the feasibility of, and need for, in situ gene banking as a complement to ex situ conservation. In discussing the historical failure to come up with "practical avenues" to achieve the in situ preservation of crop genetic resources in the developing world, Altieri and Merrick pointed out:

> This failure is understandable because preserving crop genetic resources in the midst of agricultural modernization efforts is not only a technically complicated but a politically sensitive issue. There are many economic forces that push farmers to accept newly introduced varieties. This trend has resulted not only in the disappearance of indigenous varieties, potentially useful germplasm, but has affected the social organization of peasant groups because the new varieties and their associated technologies have inevitably been accessible only to peasants most forward in terms of credit, technical assistance, and markets. (1987:92)

Against this backdrop, we can appreciate that "certain on-site, conservation strategies may play on the natural comparative advantage of marginal areas" (Brush 1991:159–160). I would like to carry this argument further by pooling our results from memory banking and in situ gene banking. Our experience points to the distinct comparative advantage of not only marginal areas within the world system or even of regions within the developing world but also of marginal farming households within each area's socioeconomic structure and, more than this, of marginal individuals within households. Marginality, in these cases, is externally defined and, to a certain extent, imposed, and has a more direct relation to centrality and power than to the actual importance of the role. It seems to me that the degree of independence, even irreverence, necessary for the nurturance and persistence of diversity is inversely proportional to the degree of integration into the market system or the degree of capture by the political vortex.

In situ gene banking is a promising channel of genetic conservation that could prove compatible with ex situ gene banking and with development if it is pursued with full regard to its historical, cultural, and institutional context. Any initiative in this direction needs to build upon indigenous practices, such as the various forms of polycultures and home gardens. Nevertheless, a certain degree of scientific input and policy support may be necessary because the encroachment on traditional farming systems of markets and agricultural extension is very real and is exceedingly powerful. Note that many of the cases cited by Altieri and Merrick (1987) in support of their argument regarding the persistence of diversity in farmers' fields were either from very remote places or from pre–Green Revolution periods (e.g., Thai and Indonesian rice farms as reported by King 1927; tomato as reported by Rick 1958; and crop-weed communities as reported by Altieri et al. 1977). We have to take account of the fact that the hegemony of modern agriculture is far more compelling today.

Brush (1991) outlined five principles for successful in situ conservation. These were: (1) complementarity with ex situ conservation efforts, (2) minimal institutional development and intervention, (3) reinforcement of existing institutions and incentives, (4) agricultural development policies that enhance farmer incentives to maintain germplasm resources, and (5) international support for conservation. Further, Brush suggested that implementation could be accomplished following four basic steps: (1) establish a clear institutional mandate specifying international centers for crop germplasm conservation, (2) establish a second international mandate designating the institution that would monitor world crop collections, including the agroecology systems where crops are grown, (3) promote the participation of national and regional agencies in in situ conservation programs to stimulate local-level participation, and (4) engage the participation of nongovernmental organizations and private voluntary organizations to establish closer ties with and better access to farmers. It must be emphasized, however, that all these principles and "steps" point to the need for *benign intervention* to support a practice that is widely recognized to *already* exist in home gardens, polycultures, and traditional agrosystems. The point is to make the conservation component more systematic, sustainable, and intrinsic and to link it to imperatives beyond the local, even regional, scale. These principles should also not detract from the fact that farmers have historically nurtured diversity in the microenvironments they control and thus may need institutional support (at the national and international level) but certainly not an institutional mandate to continue doing so.

As scientists assume a more facilitative role, however, open lines of communication must at all times be maintained with the farming populations, and the principles of local sovereignty, access, and control respected and upheld. Programs should also be flexible enough to admit and capitalize on unexpected trajectories, as in the case of female kin "rescuing" parts of the germplasm collection in Dalwangan. In other words, one cannot predetermine outcomes without ruling out unexpected possibilities that may prove to be even more worthwhile than the initial direction one set out to pursue. Finally, there should be greater sensitivity to, and appreciation of, fuzziness and marginality. Carolyn Sach's conclusion that "women's activities at the grassroots level may provide new insights and pathways to diversity— not a shallow diversity that merely emphasizes difference, end products, or biodiversity at the expense of cultural diversity and re-structuring power relations" (1992:10) is particularly relevant in this regard. Multiplicity of decision-making criteria and a certain degree of insulation from mainstreaming through commercial agriculture have been and, to a certain extent, still are effective buffers against the erosion of diversity, both biological and cultural. Finally, while more work needs to be done on the division of labor (and aptitude) between the sexes, our work indicates that women have a stronger appreciation of and inclination to preserve the diversity of plant genetic resources and are promising key players for in situ gene banking.

7

GENE-RICH BUT
TECHNOLOGY-POOR?

The Fallacy of the Equation

Memories accrue over time, sifted through eons of success, agony, and the struggles of men and women. Collective and individual memories are valued or devalued depending upon one's vantage point or the prevailing ethos of a particular moment in history. Current concerns for sustainability and equitability have introduced an increasing tension into the calculus of valuation. On the one hand, indigenous knowledge and practices are extolled because of the belief that they are low-impact and environmentally friendly, embodying age-old wisdom of how humans can live in harmony with nature. On the other hand, and this is where the irony is most palpable, they are devalued (or *un*valued) by their very value—by the argument that to treat knowledge as currency in the world system is to commodify and thereby trivialize these memories.

The main thesis of this book is that preserving local knowledge pertaining to traditional varieties of crops is complementary, and in many respects indispensable, to the maintenance of the genetic diversity of these crops (chapters 1 and 2). By comparing agricultural technologies and varietal richness in a subsistence production area to those in a relatively commercialized area, I have tried to demonstrate the threat that agricultural development— with its attendant hybrid seeds, monoculture, and high-input technologies— poses for our cultural and biological legacy (chapter 3). I noted, though, that the existence of a multiplicity of indigenous criteria that has to be satisfied by a crop or a technology is a staunch deterrent against the erosion of bio-diversity (chapter 4).

Not only can local decision making be characterized by fuzziness and surprising adaptability, it is also infused with quiet but considerable resistance and irreverence to the hegemony of uniformity and commercialization. Pockets of memories are held in the minds of local farmers—much like valued germplasm is held in trust in gene banks, except in a more dynamic way—sustaining choices, practices, and varieties that the local people have relied on and experimented with through time (chapter 5). These memories, I have tried to point out, are unevenly distributed, with their vitality most marked at the margins of a multilayered, intricately nested world system.

Ideologically, these memories poke fun at facile generalizations and challenge revered theodicies about agriculture, about development, and about the whole strategy of "empowerment" and integration. Along the same gradient, in situ germplasm conservation, in our experience, is most compatible with egalitarian, informal networks that are based on camaraderie and shared interests rather than on highly organized political structures based on authority and power (chapter 6). Moreover, in keeping with the inverse relationship between marginality and homogeneity, it appears that resistant memories, empathy toward biodiversity, and irreverence to the treadmill of monoculture are exhibited to a greater degree by subsistence farmers than commercial farmers, and more by women than by men.

If the fuzzy evaluation criteria, the irreverent pockets of memories, and the diverse farmers' home gardens were invincible by virtue of their marginality, then we would need to go no further in this discussion. The fact is, however, that the local is inextricably embedded in the global. Forces emanating from outside the "village" penetrate even the most traditional agroecosystems and thus render local frameworks passé, indigenous technologies obsolete, and farmers' landraces archaic. Vandana Shiva put this succinctly: "The change in the nature of the seed is justified by creating a framework that treats self-regenerative seed as 'primitive' and as 'raw' germplasm and the seed that is inert without inputs and non-reproducible as the finished product. The whole is rendered partial, the partial whole" (1993:287).

Thus, "elite" varieties embody elite scientific knowledge, perpetuating not only a skewed attribution of contribution but also, sadly, an extremely lopsided distribution of access and rewards. That the centers of diversity are located in the global south has long been recognized (fig. 7.1). Access to these

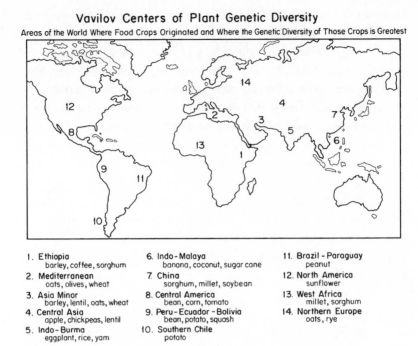

Vavilov Centers of Plant Genetic Diversity

Areas of the World Where Food Crops Originated and Where the Genetic Diversity of Those Crops is Greatest

1. Ethiopia
   barley, coffee, sorghum
2. Mediterranean
   oats, olives, wheat
3. Asia Minor
   barley, lentil, oats, wheat
4. Central Asia
   apple, chickpeas, lentil
5. Indo-Burma
   eggplant, rice, yam

6. Indo-Malaya
   banana, coconut, sugar cane
7. China
   sorghum, millet, soybean
8. Central America
   bean, corn, tomato
9. Peru-Ecuador-Bolivia
   bean, potato, squash
10. Southern Chile
    potato

11. Brazil-Paraguay
    peanut
12. North America
    sunflower
13. West Africa
    millet, sorghum
14. Northern Europe
    oats, rye

Figure 7.1. Centers of plant diversity (from Keystone Center 1991).

genetic resources by the more industrialized north has been conventionally and conveniently justified by the "common human heritage" argument, which posits that biological resources are, or should be, the legacy of all humankind. Although this argument is almost intuitively right, the breakdown of the commons perspective came about with the granting of plant patents for products of plant breeding and, much later, biotechnology. The Plant Patent Act of 1930 statutorily recognized that plant breeders created products that were more than products of nature. Recently this patent protection has been extended to "discoverers" of eligible material, thus covering every variety that can be demonstrated to possess a sufficiently distinct combination of unique characteristics (Jondle 1989; Sealy 1993). This obviously puts small-scale farmers who have nurtured, bred, and experimented with landraces all their lives but know little about the legal system at a distinct disadvantage. As Roy Pat Mooney pointed out:

> From one perspective, both IARCS (International Agricultural Research Centers) and Third World farmers could and should take

pride in their contribution to global agriculture. In principle, there is no reason why the North should not benefit. The problem arises when the commercial value flowing North is not acknowledged and not compensated. The situation is seriously aggravated when northern governments allow the patenting of material wholly or partially derived from farmers' varieties. As private companies move into Third World seed markets, farmers are finding themselves paying for the product of their own genius. (1993:178)

In the 1980s, the "beneficial exchange" principle gained currency to rationalize the flow of genetic resources from centers of diversity in less developed or developing countries to centers of conservation and profitable use in developed countries. The shorthand for this principle is as follows: by virtue of the global south being "gene-rich but technology-poor" and the global north being "gene-poor but technology-rich," the maintenance of an exchange mechanism that would facilitate the flow of germplasm from south to north, reciprocated by a flow of knowledge and technology in the opposite direction, is not only beneficial but is also necessary to both. Happily, this should create a climate of well-adjusted codependence. This is still another case, however, wherein the myth of "the emperor's new clothes" assumes a life of its own and its reality is never questioned. It is only by conceiving technology through a very narrow lens as a *system of doing* that is generated, validated, and legitimized by Western science that the above equation can be sustained. As the present work and others before it have taken pains to show, local technologies that are sustainable, context sensitive, compatible with local opportunities and constraints, and responsive to a variety of demands flourish in farming communities and in fact undergird much of the diversity preserved in farmers' fields.

With the common human heritage argument down, and the gene-rich/technology-poor equation wobbly, one must grapple with the question of why germplasm and associated knowledge should flow at all instead of being tightly guarded in restricted enclaves. A related question that is particularly relevant to memory banking concerns knowledge. Should indigenous agricultural knowledge remain above commodification in order to avoid capitalistic pitfalls, as Stephen Brush (1994) contended, or should local populations proactively capture the market bull—which will get them one way or another anyway—by the horns and make themselves its master?

In my view, the flow of germplasm and associated knowledge is not inherently or necessarily exploitative. In fact, such a flow—along with the associated compensation potential—will enhance local pride in, and vigilance over, plant genetic resources and, as a consequence, promote conservation through use. For reasons I need not further belabor, indigenous knowledge and practices must be documented soon by whoever is (individually or institutionally) sincerely willing to undertake the effort before all is lost. Each generation of experts, of local farmers, passes away and takes along an irretrievable store of knowledge. In addition, I am wary of arguments that simply scuttle efforts at attribution and compensation in relation to both germplasm and knowledge. The position that landraces and associated technologies are products of collective, communal, and intergenerational effort and therefore beyond "authorship" and proprietary rights begs the question for the simple reason that science is exactly the same way—building by accretion and communication, by standing on the shoulders of intellectual ancestors—and yet this has not posed any insurmountable impediments to the patenting of its products. Jack Kloppenburg went right to the heart of the matter when he wrote:

> Rarely are landraces attributable to an individual, a particular time, or a particular location. Similarly, today, many new varieties are the product of a corporate endeavor and not truly traceable to a single breeder. Thus, when discussing Plant Breeders' Rights, we are concerned about the rights of a corporate entity, while in the case of Farmers' Rights we are concerned with farmers *as a class*. In the former case, it is relatively easy to pay royalties to a seed company, for example. In the latter, however, there is no reason why payment to nations in the form of conserving germplasm and building effective plant breeding programs cannot be carried out. Put another way, there is no reason why free access must mean access without compensation. (1990:122)

The global genetic resources system, it has been said, is immersed in a competition-cooperation paradox among nations in control of resources (Lacy 1995). Negotiations about farmers' rights, defined by the 1989 FAO Conference resolution as "rights arising from the past, present, and future contributions of farmers in conserving, improving, and making available plant genetic resources" vis-à-vis plant breeders' rights, while healthy and urgently needed, could take attention away from the equally pressing task of conservation of genetic and cultural diversity that demands collaboration at all levels. We are in a particularly vulnerable period because recent technological advancements and legal/political developments could seriously plunge us into genetic erosion and cultural (dis)integration. As Lawrence Busch noted:

> It has been argued that extension of utility patents to plants is likely to encourage greater uniformity in the field as breeders respond to legal rather than agronomic or scientific breeding requirements. For example, the uniformity and stability required by PVPA (the Plant Variety Protection Act) is not connected to agronomic needs. . . . Moreover, even the registrations under the PVPA have been limited to just a few widely grown crops and there is no evidence to suggest that overall R&D occurred as a result of that law. Smaller markets for many fruit and vegetable crops may well be ignored as the cost of research outweighs the profits to be derived by both the private and public sectors. (1993:122–123)

One contribution that memory banking can make to the conservation of biodiversity is that it will not allow us to forget that options are available, that viable alternatives have existed throughout time and space, and that local evaluation criteria—in addition to agronomic and scientific ones—are important and need to be seriously considered. The key is to document agricultural knowledge in such a way that the local population has the ultimate control over access—so that the *authors* who possess the copyright will have a say in determining the terms of sharing and exchange. In this manner, they can utilize conventions that exist in the global marketplace to their advantage instead of being talked about and talked over in intersectoral negotiations and international forums that are supposedly for their welfare. Work is continuing in this direction, as exemplified by the Memory Web, a "layered" data base for memory banking research and networking that is currently online in the World Wide Web (http://www/uga.edu/~ebl). Eventually, the Memory Web will be an interactive data base that will involve scientists and local farmers in the systematic documentation, conservation, and exchange of local knowledge pertaining to plant genetic resources. A complementary activity that is being initiated by the Ethnoecology/Biodiversity Laboratory at the University of Georgia is youth-led memory banking, wherein local youth are trained in recording and preserving the knowledge of their elders (see Nazarea et al. 1997).

In the meantime, I am reminded of a line from a Bukidnon epic, the *Olaging*: "If we pass there / This we shall pass / This we shall traverse again." Hopefully, the path—or paths—will be intact when humanity finds a need or desire to retrace some of its steps or guide its new directions. We should take our cue from the Bukidnons, who knew that varieties and memories, if conserved and transmitted, can link us solidly to our past and transport us sanely to our future.

APPENDIX A

Indigenous Beliefs and Practices Associated with Sweet Potato Cultivation among Farmers in Bukidnon

Stage in Agricultural Cycle	Beliefs and Practices	Location		
		Kaamulan[1]	Intavas	Salvacion
Land preparation				
Tools	Use sharpened sticks of wood or bamboo in cultivating the soil.	●		
	Use a long-bladed knife (bolo) and grab hoe (bigkong or piko) in cultivating the soil.		●	●
	Use a carabao-drawn plow to clear/cultivate an area which is flat; use knives for hilly or sloping areas.		●	●
Methods	Loosen the soil up to three inches deep only before the cuttings are planted.	●		
	Sometimes use the slash-and-burn method for clearing the area.		●	●
	Summer is the best time to clear the area; grasses dry faster and are easier to burn.		●	
	Follow clearing/cleaning the area by pulverizing the soil.			●
	Furrow and hill-up the soil prior to planting.		●	●

[1] The Kaamulan Festival is an annual gathering of the indigenous populations of Bukidnon. The first series of informal interviews, elicitation of life histories, and collection of local drawings of traditional varieties was done during the 1989 Kaamulan Festival. The results are included here to round out the picture and to serve as another point of comparison—some of the ethnic groups that participate in the Kaamulan Festival are even less integrated into the market system than the natives of Intavas.

Stage in Agricultural Cycle	Beliefs and Practices	Location		
		Kaamulan[1]	Intavas	Salvacion
Planting				
Tools	A long-bladed knife (*bolo*) and other metal implements can be used in planting.	●	●	●
Timing	Plant during the start of the lunar cycle (new moon) at the break of dawn in order to have a good harvest.		●	●
	Plant during the full moon when the clouds are rounded to ensure an abundant harvest.	●	●	●
	Plant during the full moon so the roots will be big and plentiful.	●	●	●
	Plant when the moon is big and there are plenty of stars in the sky so the sweet potatoes will have many roots.	●	●	●
	Plant when the moon is full because the sea will also be swollen and there will be many shells left on the shore; hence, sweet potatoes will also have many roots.			●
	Plant three to five days after the full moon to have a good harvest.	●		●

Stage in Agricultural Cycle	Beliefs and Practices	Location		
		Kaamulan[1]	Intavas	Salvacion
Planting (*continued*)				
Timing (*continued*)	Plant when the moon can be seen during the daytime so that, like the moon, the roots will be seen any-time, anywhere.	●		
	Plant during the last quarter so insects will not see the plants and the roots will not rot.	●		
	Plant during the last quarter when the tide is low; at this time many rocks and stones are exposed near the sea, so sweet potatoes will have many roots.			●
	Never plant when the moon is full because rats will attack the plants.		●	
	Low tide is deter-mined by looking at the eyeball of a cat. If the pupil is small, it is low tide; if it is big, it is high tide.			●
	Never plant when it is low tide because there will be few roots.			●
	Plant in the morning for the best harvest.	●		
	The best time to plant is on Sunday at sunset.	●		

Stage in Agricultural Cycle	Beliefs and Practices	Location		
		Kaamulan[1]	Intavas	Salvacion
	Plant at night when it is very dark so pests will not attack the plant.		●	
	Never plant on a day which has an *r*, for example, *Martes* (Tuesday). Instead, choose a day that has no *r*, like *Sabado* (Saturday) or *linggo* (Sunday).			●
	January to April is the best time for planting; never plant in May because it is the start of the rainy season and the roots will rot.	●	●	
	Start planting in October or November since this is the beginning of the dry season; hence, there will be plenty of roots.			●
	Plant in November so there will be as many roots as there are heads in the cemetery during All Saints' Day.			●
	Never plant in May; because of the frequent rains, only the leaves will keep growing.			●
	Plant sweet potato right after potato.		●	
	Sweet potato is best planted right after corn.		●	

Stage in Agricultural Cycle	Beliefs and Practices	Location		
		Kaamulan[1]	Intavas	Salvacion
Planting (*continued*)				
Timing (*continued*)	Alternate, planting sweet potato with to-mato so that the roots of the sweet potatoes will grow big from leftover fertilizer and chicken dung applied to the tomato.			●
Source of planting material	Given by, or ex-changed with, neighbors.	●	●	
	Obtained from elders of the community.		●	●
	Obtained from origi-nal settlers of the community.		●	●
	Exchanged with farmers from other municipalities (*baranggays*).			●
	Obtained from other natives across the mountains.	●		
Methods	Say a prayer before planting so the roots will not be damaged by pests.		●	
	The hills should be well spaced so there is enough room for roots to grow before they overlap; other-wise the sweet pota-toes will just keep producing leaves.	●	●	
	Roots grow bigger when sweet potatoes		●	

Stage in Agricultural Cycle	Beliefs and Practices	Location		
		Kaamulan[1]	Intavas	Salvacion
	are planted in a sloping area because the soil is more fertile; soil on a plain becomes compressed easily.			
	Bite the vines before planting so a lot of roots will be produced.	●		
	Tie the cuttings into knots before planting so the roots will cluster in only one area.	●		
	Plant four to six cuttings, each about a foot long, per hill, with ends facing each other.	●		
	Plant with traditional rituals such as kneeling and covering each newly planted hill with all ten fingers so the cuttings underneath will produce as many roots.		●	●
	Kneel over newly planted materials with both knees and both elbows touching the ground to induce the formation of large roots.			●
Materials mixed with cuttings	Mix hair and *buri* mat with planting materials while praying for the roots to be as many as the strands of hair or mat.	●		●

Stage in Agricultural Cycle	Beliefs and Practices	Location		
		Kaamulan[1]	Intavas	Salvacion

Planting (continued)
  Materials mixed
  with cuttings
  (continued)
	Mix broomstick with cuttings so there will be as many roots as there are "sticks."		•	•

	Collect grasses under the house to mix with planting materials so there will be many roots.	•		
	Burn grasses and dry leaves and mix the ashes with the cuttings so there will be many roots.		•	
	Mix thorns of cogon grass and rattan with planting materials to induce the formation of many roots and to make the roots cluster in one area, respectively.			•
	Mix a weed that bears many fruits (karogom) with the cuttings so the sweet potatoes will have many roots.		•	
	Mix the bark of a tree with many roots (iba) with cuttings while praying so that the sweet potatoes have as many roots as the iba.	•		
	Mix the bark of a fruit tree that bears many fruits (balingbing)	•		

Stage in Agricultural Cycle	Beliefs and Practices	Location		
		Kaamulan[1]	Intavas	Salvacion
	with planting materials so there will be many roots.			
	Mix the bark of a tree that has many thorns (*sampinit*) with cuttings so there will be many roots.		•	
	Include the bark of any tree so the sweet potatoes will have as many roots as the branches of a tree.		•	
	Include the fruit of a tree that has many roots (*tubog*) for a good harvest.			•
	Mix banana stalks (pedicels) and ashes with cuttings to promote the clustering of roots and a powdery texture, respectively.			•
	Mix ginger and peanuts with planting materials for weevil resistance and for a good harvest, respectively.			•
	Include snails with planting materials so the roots will cluster in one area.			•
	Include a salamander (*tuko*) so the roots will be elongated.			•

Stage in Agricultural Cycle	Beliefs and Practices	Location		
		Kaamulan[1]	Intavas	Salvacion
Planting (continued) Materials mixed with cuttings (continued)	Mix snake bones with cuttings so the sweet potatoes will have as many roots as the bones of a snake.	●		
	Include a portion of the house post so the roots will grow long.			●
	Mix holy water with some cuttings so God will watch over and protect the crop.			●
Gender of the one who plants	Elderly females should be the ones to plant since they are more familiar with tradi-tional beliefs and practices.			●
	Females should plant since it is an easy job and the sweet potato plot is near the house.		●	
	Males should plant and should be naked so the harvest will be good.			
	Males should plant since they know the beliefs and traditions to be followed.			●
	Males should plant since they are stronger.		●	
	Males should plant since females do the household chores.			●

Stage in Agricultural Cycle	Beliefs and Practices	Location		
		Kaamulan[1]	Intavas	Salvacion
	Either the male or the female can plant as long as he/she knows how to do it.		●	●
	Both male and female can plant.	●		
Cultural management				
Crop maintenance	Cover creeping vines with soil so they will produce roots also.	●	●	●
	While weeding, trim off the tops of the plants so they will have more roots and will not die easily.		●	
Fertilizing	Allow grasses that come from the field to rot and then plow them in to enrich the soil.			●
	Do not use chemicals, especially for sweet potatoes.			
Weeding	Cut grasses and weeds using a scythe (sanggot) or a long-bladed knife (bolo) to maintain the cleanliness of the area.		●	●
	Burn weeds so they will not grow back rapidly.		●	
	A plow can also be used for weeding.		●	
	Weed only once during the entire planting season.			●

Stage in Agricultural Cycle	Beliefs and Practices	Location		
		Kaamulan[1]	Intavas	Salvacion
Cultural management (*continued*)				
Pest control	Leave rats to eat as much as they can since they cannot eat everything anyway.		●	
	Allow insects and other pests to eat as much as they can eat because if they are "touched" they will become more angry and will damage everything in the field.			●
	Say prayers to the gods (e.g., the god of rats) while walking around to implore them to spare/protect one's fields.		●	●
	Offer gifts of food (e.g., chicken, eggs, candies, soft drinks, and bread) and make sacrifices to the spirits so they will protect the crops from pests.		●	●
	The first harvest should not be broiled, just boiled, so that insects and other pests will not damage the remaining roots.	●		
	Don't time planting so that roots will mature during summer because there will be a lot of weevils to attack the roots then.			●
	Cleaning the area from time to time by		●	●

Stage in Agricultural Cycle	Beliefs and Practices	Location		
		Kaamulan[1]	Intavas	Salvacion
	cutting the weeds will prevent rats from entering the field.			
	Collect worms and caterpillars and burn them in a can so that the pests will not attack the crops anymore.	●		
	Harvest weevil-infested roots immediately and keep them in one corner of the house.		●	
	Completely cover the roots with soil to prevent weevils from damaging them.			●
	Place locally made rat traps (*bulakan*) constructed out of wood/bamboo in different parts of the field.		●	
	Tie strips of cellophane or any white material to poles and place these in different parts of the field to scare the rats.		●	
Harvesting				
Tools	Use a stick or sharpened wood around 12 inches in length (*lub-ang* or *kali*) for harvesting so that vines and smaller roots won't be damaged.	●	●	●

Stage in Agricultural Cycle	Beliefs and Practices	Location		
		Kaamulan[1]	Intavas	Salvacion
Harvesting (*continued*)				
Tools (*continued*)	Never use a long-bladed knife (*bolo*) in harvesting, for it will damage vines and smaller roots.	●	●	●
	Use a knife (*bolo*) in harvesting so weeding can be done at the same time.			●
Methods	Harvest on a staggered basis, getting the big roots only as needed and leaving the smaller ones to grow; this way, the sweet potatoes will not die and will continue producing roots (may last for a year).	●	●	●
	Harvest only two roots per hill so that the other roots will continue to grow and there will be something to harvest the next month.			●
	Harvest all roots simultaneously if the soil is fertile; otherwise, harvest the big ones first.	●		
	Harvest on time (i.e., four months after planting) so that the roots will not rot.		●	
	Roots that are coming out of the soil should	●		

Stage in Agricultural Cycle	Beliefs and Practices	Location		
		Kaamulan[1]	Intavas	Salvacion
	be harvested at once so that they will not rot.			
	Kill a chicken and offer it to the gods in thanksgiving for a good harvest.	●		
	Offer eggs to the gods for the roots to be powdery. Sometimes, sugar cane is also offered for the roots to be sweet.	●	●	
	Say prayers before harvesting to ask permission of the gods and to thank them for a good harvest.		●	●
	Call upon *Magkabaya Bagulado* to shower his grace on the harvest.			●
	Harvest only three roots on the first day to show respect for the other "beings."			●
	The first harvested roots should not be eaten.		●	
	Say prayers before the harvested roots are eaten.		●	
	The first harvested roots should not be broiled so that the roots left in the field will not be damaged by weevils.		●	

Stage in Agricultural Cycle	Beliefs and Practices	Location		
		Kaamulan[1]	Intavas	Salvacion
Harvesting (*continued*)				
Methods (*continued*)	The first three harvested roots should be broiled, then rubbed with the ashes and eaten by the husband so that the roots left in the field will become powdery and will not be attacked by weevils.			●
	Rub the first root that is harvested with sugar and ashes before cooking; this is to make the remaining roots sweet and powdery.		●	
Gender of the one who harvests	Never allow the male to do the harvesting or he will thereafter behave like a wild boar.	●		
	The female does the harvesting because she values the importance of farm work.		●	
	The female harvests because it is an easy job.		●	
	The female should harvest because it is the male who does the clearing and the planting.		●	
	The female household head does the harvesting because she		●	

Stage in Agricultural Cycle	Beliefs and Practices	Location		
		Kaamulan[1]	Intavas	Salvacion
	knows when and how to do it.			
	Males harvest and eat the first three roots; this way, the rest of the roots become dry and powdery.			●
	Females should not harvest because, if they do, the roots will be attacked by weevils.			●
	Females are not allowed to walk around the field during their period because, if they do, weevils will attack the sweet potatoes.			●
	Whoever did the planting should also do the harvesting.		●	
	Either males or females can harvest.		●	
Storage	Stagger the harvest and store roots underground until they are needed.		●	
	Roots are not stored because they are consumed or sold immediately after harvest.			●
	Roots can be stored to ripen for three days to one week as long as they were not damaged during harvesting.	●	●	

Stage in Agricultural Cycle	Beliefs and Practices	Location		
		Kaamulan[1]	Intavas	Salvacion
Harvesting (*continued*)				
Storage (*continued*)	Never store damaged roots, because they rot easily; they should be cooked immediately.	●	●	
	Do not wash the roots that will be stored, because the skin will dry up and break when exposed to the sun.	●	●	
	Harvested roots that are not consumed should be covered with dried leaves.	●		
	Allow "excess" roots to dry outside for one day and then place them in a storage basket (*bukog* or *buda*).	●		
	Allow "excess" roots to ripen in one corner of the house where air can freely circulate, never in a storeroom; these can last for up to two weeks.	●	●	
	Keep "excess" roots in a sack; one can just get the roots from the sack as needed.		●	
	Place "excess" roots in an underground pit lined with leaves, cellophane, or sacks and topped with a layer of soil.			●

Stage in Agricultural Cycle	Beliefs and Practices	Location		
		Kaamulan[1]	Intavas	Salvacion
	Slice "excess" roots into smaller pieces and dry in the sun; dried chips can last for months.	●		●
Utilization	Sweet potato roots can be used as a staple in the absence of rice or corn, or as a dish in the absence of meat or fish.	●	●	●
	Roots are sold in the market or on the farm itself.		●	●
	Feed roots, especially those damaged by weevils, to chickens and pigs. Leaves can also be fed to farm animals.		●	●
	As human food, roots can be boiled, broiled, fried in oil, or cooked as porridge (*lugaw*), soup (*tinabi-rak*), or dessert (*binig-nit*, *suman*, *kidkiron*, and *bitso-bitso*).	●	●	●
	Planting more than one variety allows farmers to have a wide range of choices regarding what varieties they feel like eating.			●
	Give broiled roots to sick people to make them strong; roots relieve severe hunger		●	●

Stage in Agricultural Cycle	Beliefs and Practices	Location		
		Kaamulan[1]	Intavas	Salvacion
Harvesting (*continued*) Utilization (*continued*)	pangs (*tambal sa gutom*).	●	●	●
	Leaves are consumed as a side dish (sometimes with roots as a staple) or as salad.	●	●	●
	Leaves can be boiled and filtered and the remaining solution mixed with local lemon (*kalamansi*) and sugar to make *camote* juice.			●
	Use leaves to relieve stomach disorders; i.e., by placing broiled leaves directly on the navel.		●	
	Use leaves to heal skin disease such as *bubag*, and to relieve itchy skin.		●	●
	Place leaves on the the belly of a woman who is about to deliver her baby; this can help make delivery easy.			●
	Use sweet potato tops in curing allergic reactions to fish and cassava, such as headaches and nausea (symptoms of food poisoning).			●

APPENDIX B

Benchmark Socioeconomic Survey Interview Schedule

HOUSEHOLD SURVEY DATA

Household Number:

Nearest Neighbors:

Name of Interviewer:

Date:

Time:

1. Household members' names, role, age, sex, occupation, educational attainment?
2. Length of residence in the area, number of years or months?
3. Place of origin, migration history?
4. Size of land being cultivated?
5. Crops planted and area utilized for each crop?
6. Crops planted in home garden, if any?
7. Land utilized for sweet potato production, if any?
8. Length of experience in planting sweet potatoes?
9. Varieties planted and characteristics of each?
10. Proportion of produce for consumption and for sale?
11. Other varieties known, though not necessarily planted, and their characteristics?
12. Neighbors and other villagers who are known to have been planting sweet potatoes for a long time?
13. Neighbors and other villagers who are known to be knowledgeable about different sweet potato varieties?
14. Reasons for not planting sweet potatoes?
15. Characteristics of newly introduced sweet potato varieties, if any?

NOTES AND COMMENTS BASED ON GENERAL OBSERVATION

1. Type of housing material: concrete / wood / thatch
2. General state of house: relatively new / old but well-maintained / dilapidated
3. General state of health of household members: good health / poor health / weak and sickly
4. Appliances: refrigerator / TV / electric or gas stove / cassette tape / other
5. Willingness to be interviewed: very willing / complies reluctantly / not willing

APPENDIX C

Triads Test Items

TRIADS TEST (SALVACION)

Instructions: *Which one of the three items/varieties is different from the other two? Why?*

1. klarin/kasindol/igorot
2. kamada/kinampay/5-finger
3. tinangkong/valencia/kabato
4. buwan-buwan/amerikano/laguitlit
5. arabia/kabohol/katibor
6. katimpa/dalian/tapol
7. kalinggatos/imelda/sil-ipon
8. klarin/kasindol/katapok
9. kasindol/igorot/katapok
10. sil-ipon/kamada/kinampay
11. tapol/katibor/valencia
12. laguitlit/buwan-buwan/katibor
13. kabohol/arabia/klarin
14. katimpa/5-finger/dalian
15. imelda/kalinggatos/tinangkong

TRIADS TEST (INTAVAS)

Instructions: *Which one of the three items/varieties is different from the other two?*

1. lambayong/valencia/siuron
2. kamba/malaybalay/initlog
3. lamputi/kulating/kauyag
4. imelda/tinangkong/5-finger

5. kalugti/manobo/dinagat
6. arabia/gireng-gireng/ubihon
7. siquijor/kalibre/turay
8. amerikano/siñorita/lawaton
9. kabus-ok/hinapon/sabat
10. lambayong/laguitas/siuron
11. valencia/laguitas/lambayong
12. initlog/hinapon/malaybalay
13. kauyag/amerikano/kulating
14. kalibre/5-finger/tinangkong
15. dinagat/arabia/kalugti
16. gireng-gineng/si-uron/ubihon
17. siquijor/lawaton/lamputi
18. siñorita/lawaton/lamputi
19. imelda/kabus-ok/sabat

APPENDIX D

Local Evaluations of Sweet Potato Varieties
in Bukidnon

Local Varietal[1] Name	Location/Source	Morphological Characteristics	Growth Habit	Postharvest Characteristics	Gastronomic Characteristics	Uses
Amerikano	Intavas and Salvacion	White/red skin, yellow/white flesh, big, elongated root, big green leaves, red tops.	Produces many leaves but few roots; dies easily.		Sweet, powdery.	Good for home consumption.
Andes	Intavas	Red skin, yellow flesh.	Produces many roots.	Ripens in 6 days.	Sweet, powdery.	Good for home consumption.
Baksalan	Impasug-ong (Bukidnon tribe)	Yellow skin, yellow flesh.				
Bakson	Impasug-ong	White skin, yellow flesh, elongated roots.	Vine does not creep/spread.		Not so dry, not so sweet.	Good for home consumption, used in making *benignit*.[2]
Balidbid	Sinuda, Kitao-Tao (Matigsalog tribe)	Red skin, small, elongated roots.			Very powdery, roots are sweet when cooked.	
Bara-bara	Guilang-Guilang Manolo Fortich (Bukidnon tribe), and Sungco, Lantapan (Talaandig tribe)	Yellow/white skin, white flesh, big, elongated roots, green leaves.	Does not produce many roots; vines also produce roots.	Takes one week to ripen.	Bland, powdery.	Used as porridge for sick people.

Variety	Description	Growing characteristics	Ripening	Taste	Uses
Binawil (Binawin, Binawon)	White skin, white flesh, elongated roots, green leaves.	Should be planted when the moon is big.		Sweet/bland, not so powdery.	Good for home consumption.
Bulakaw (Initlog)	Yellow skin, yellow flesh, rounded, egg-shaped roots, rounded leaves, green tops.	Produces few roots, both vines and base of plant produce roots, takes 4 months to mature.	Takes one week to ripen.	Bland, powdery.	Good for home consumption.
Butigo	Violet/black skin, violet flesh, serrated, rounded leaves, black vines.				
Dalurong, Kitao-tao (Manobo tribe)					
Dalian (Siuron, Kamada)	Red/white skin, yellow/white flesh, big, elongated roots, white leaves, violet tops.	Produces roots within short period, roots grow at the base of plant, takes 3 months to mature, hardy.	Takes 3–7 days to ripen, rots easily.	Sweet, watery/powdery.	Good for camote fritter, for home consumption, saleable in the market.
Salvacion and Intavas					
Dinagat	Pink/red skin, white flesh, big, rounded, elongated root, flat, wide, rounded, yellow/green leaves.	Produces many roots, takes 6 months to mature, vines also produce roots.		Sweet, very powdery.	Good for home consumption, as animal feed, saleable in the market.
Intavas and Salvacion					

[1] Varietal names that are enclosed in parentheses were given by other informants but consensus seemed to center around the first name listed.

[2] "Benignit" is a local sweetish snack consisting of sliced sweet potatoes mixed with other root crops and simmered in coconut milk until tender.

[3] "Camote cue" is a snack made by frying sweet potato slices with brown sugar, then the syrup-coated slices are skewered on a bamboo stick.

[4] "Tinabirak" is a porridge made by stirring grated sweet potatoes in boiling water until pulp is dispersed in the broth.

[5] "Suman" is a native delicacy made with sweet potato flour wrapped in banana leaves and steamed until fully cooked.

Local Varietal[1] Name	Location / Source	Morphological Characteristics	Growth Habit	Postharvest Characteristics	Gastronomic Characteristics	Uses
Five-Finger (Kawindol, Tinangkong, Arabia, Kalibre)	Salvacion and Intavas	Brown/pink/red skin, white/yellow flesh, big, rounded roots, serrated leaves, red tops.	Takes 3 months to mature, can withstand stresses (does not die easily), does not produce roots at all seasons, vines also produce roots.	Takes 5 days to ripen.	Very sweet, watery, does not crack when cooked.	Leaves are used as a vegetable, saleable in the market, good for *camote cue*.[3]
Gabanon	Dalurong, Kitao-tao (Manobo tribe)	White/orange skin, white flesh, elongated roots.	Produces many roots.			
Gireng-gireng	Intavas	White/yellow skin, small roots, serrated leaves.	Produces many roots/produces few roots, hardy (does not die easily), takes 6 months to mature.		Bland, powdery.	Leaves are used as a vegetable.
Guti (Goti)	Impasug-ong, Malaybalay (Bukidnon tribe) and Intavas	White/red skin, white flesh, rounded, white leaves, small, rounded roots.	Produces many roots, takes 4 months to mature.	Does not ripen.	Sweet, powdery, skin peels off when cooked.	Good for home consumption.
Igorot	Salvacion	Off-white/white skin, yellow/cream/white	Produces roots at the base of plant.		Delicious, sweet, not so powdery.	Good for home consumption,

Variety	Location (tribe)	Physical description	Growth characteristics	Storage/ripening	Taste	Uses
		flesh, rounded, elongated roots, small green/red leaves.				saleable in the market, used in camote cue, given to others on credit.
Imelda	Intavas, Salvacion, Dalurong, Kitao-tao (Manobo tribe)	Pink/white/yellow skin, white flesh, small, elongated roots, green/yellow leaves.	Dies easily, produces more leaves than roots, produces many roots.		Bland, not delicious.	Leaves are used as a vegetable.
Inampay (Kinampay, Ubihon)	Intavas	Violet/red skin, violet flesh, big, round, elongated roots, dark, violet, flat leaves.	Produces many roots at the base of plant, produces many leaves and vines, produces few roots, leaves are spreading/creeping.	Takes one week to ripen.	Bland/sweet, not so powdery.	Good for home consumption, used in benignit making.
Initlog (Bulakaw)	Intavas and Salvacion	Yellow/white/orange skin, yellow flesh where the core is violet and the periphery is white, rounded roots, green or light green leaves, dark green vines.	Susceptible to weevils, produces many vines but few roots, vines also produce roots, takes 3–4 months to mature.	Can be stored for one month.	Sweet, powdery, does not cause colic.	Good for broiling and good for camote cue, good for home consumption.
Kabantuk	Sinuda, Kitao-tao (Matigsalog tribe)	Red skin, yellow flesh, tiny orange root on the surface of the storage root.				

Local Varietal[1] Name	Location/ Source	Morphological Characteristics	Growth Habit	Postharvest Characteristics	Gastronomic Characteristics	Uses
Kabato (Siñorita)	Salvacion	Red/yellow/white skin, white/yellow flesh, rounded, elongated roots, serrated, three-finger, green leaves, green tops like rocks.	Produces many roots, but produces roots at the base of plant only, takes 3–4 months to mature.		Bland/very sweet, very powdery.	Leaves are used as vegetables, good substitute for bread or rice, saleable in the market.
Kabohol (Magtuko)	Salvacion	White skin, yellow/ white flesh, rounded, egg-shaped roots, small, rounded leaves.	Produces many roots, roots are produced in clusters, hardy (will last for two years), vines also produce roots/vines do not produce roots, takes 3–4 months to mature.	Takes 2–4 days to ripen, does not rot easily.	Bland/sweet, powdery, tastes just right.	Served as side dish good for home consumption.
Kabulungan (Linggatos)	Sungco, Lantapan (Talaandig tribe)	Red/yellow/white skin, white flesh, big, rounded, elongated roots, flat green leaves, red tops.	Produces roots within short period of time (three months), produces many roots/ produces few but big roots, takes 3–4 months to mature.	Takes one week to ripen.	Bland/sweet, watery/ powdery.	Good for home consumption, used in making camote cue.
Kabus-ok	Intavas and Salvacion	Yellow skin, yellow flesh, red leaves, has "canals" on the surface of the storage roots.	Produces many roots.		Powdery, bland.	Good to serve with meals.

Kabutho	Guilang-guilang, Manolo Fortich (Bukidnon tribe), and Salvacion	White skin, white/yellow flesh, rounded roots.			Very powdery, not so sweet when newly harvested but sweetens as it ripens (3 days).	Can be used as substitute for rice, good with salted fish or shrimps.
Kahul-us (Kahul-is)	Sungco, Lantapan (Talaandig tribe), Intavas	White/red skin, white flesh, elongated roots, red tops, white vines.	Produces many roots.		Skin cracks and peels off when cooked.	
Kalasano	Katablaran, Cabanglasan (Ukayamnon tribe)	Red skin, white flesh.	Wild noncultivated variety.	Takes one week to ripen.	Powdery.	
Kalibre (Five-finger, Tinangkong)	Intavas	Red/dirty white/orange skin, white/yellow flesh, big, elongated roots, flat leaves.	Produces many roots, produces roots within a short period of time, not good to cultivate during dry season, does not produce roots during all seasons, roots cluster at the base of plant, takes 3½ months to mature.	Ripens in 3–7 days.	Sweet, watery, does not crack when cooked.	Leaves are used as a vegetable, saleable in the market, good for frying.

Local Varietal[1] Name	Location/Source	Morphological Characteristics	Growth Habit	Postharvest Characteristics	Gastronomic Characteristics	Uses
Kalugti	Salvacion, Intavas, and Sungco, Lantapan (Talaandig tribe)	Yellow/white/red/brown skin, cream/yellow/white flesh, elongated, small straight/curvy roots, white/light green rounded, three-finger small leaves, small vines.	Produces roots at the base of plant, needs longer time to mature vines also produce roots, takes 3–4 months to mature.	Needs longer period to ripen.	Bland/sweet, very powdery, skin peels off when cooked, easy to slice/"hard" flesh.	Good for home consumption, especially for soup and ice candy, good for boiling, fed to pigs, saleable in the market.
Kamada	Salvacion	White skin, yellow/white flesh, elongated, big/small roots, green leaves.	Produces many roots grows quickly, vines also produce roots.		Bland, watery/powdery.	
Kamba	Dalwangan, Intavas	Red skin, yellow flesh, big, rounded roots, large vines.	Produces many roots, weevil-resistant, produces many leaves.	Takes one week to ripen.	Bland/sweet when ripened, sweeter if mature, watery.	Good for camote cue, saleable in market.
Kandulit	Katablaran, Cabanglasan (Umayamnon tribe), Silae, Cabanglasan (Bukidnon tribe), and Intavas	Red skin, white flesh, big roots.	Produces few roots.		Bland, watery.	Good for tinabirak.[4]

Kapayas	Sungco, Lantapan (Talaandig tribe), Sinuda, Kitao-tao (Matigsalog tribe), and Guilang-guilang, Monolo Fortich (Bukidnon tribe)	White skin, white flesh, big, elongated, rounded roots, green, serrated/flat, big leaves, has "canals" on the surface of storage roots.	Takes 3 months to mature, produces many roots.	Takes 2–3 days to ripen, can be stored for 7 months.	Sweet, watery, not so powdery, will not cause any stomach disorder.	Good for sick people, for home consumption.
Karunsing	Salvacion	White/violet/red/yellow with pink pigmentation skin, yellow/violet/white flesh, rounded/elongated, big/regular size roots, green leaves, red tops.	Produces many roots, takes 3½–4 months to mature, vines also produce roots, roots crack when overly mature.	Takes 4 days to ripen.	Very sweet, very powdery.	Good for *tinabirak, benignit, camote fritter, camote cue,* and saleable in the market.
Kasindol	Salvacion	Red skin, yellow flesh, elongated, regular size, clean roots.	New variety, early maturing.		Sweet, watery/very dry, does not crack when cooked, very delicious.	Good for *camote cue,* saleable in market, most popular variety in Salvacion.
Katabang	Kitao-tao	Red skin, yellow flesh, green leaves, violet tops.	Takes 3 months to mature.	Can be stored for one month as long as it is kept in an underground pit.	Sweet, powdery, not soggy.	Saleable in the market, good for home consumption.

Local Varietal[1] Name	Location/ Source	Morphological Characteristics	Growth Habit	Postharvest Characteristics	Gastronomic Characteristics	Uses
Katibor	Salvacion	White skin, white flesh, rounded roots, big, light green leaves.	Roots grow at the base of the plant, produces roots easily, dies easily.	Takes one week to ripen.	Sweet, powdery/watery.	Good for home consumption.
Katimpa	Salvacion	Yellow skin, yellow flesh, big roots, serrated leaves.	Roots only grow at the base of plant.		Bland/sweet.	Good for home consumption.
Katuka (Katuko, Lambayong)	Salvacion	White/red skin, white flesh, rounded roots, green, rounded, heart-shaped leaves, red tops.	Takes 4 months to mature, produces many roots, weevil-resistant.	Takes one week to ripen.	Sweet/bland, very powdery/ not so powdery.	Good to blend/ mix with coffee, good for suman,[5] for home consumption/not recommended for home consumption.
Kaulog	Don Carlos	Yellow skin, yellow flesh, rounded roots, rounded leaves.	Takes 8 months to mature, produces many roots.	Does not ripen.	Sweet, powdery.	Good for home consumption.
Kauyag	Sungco, Lantapan (Talaandig tribe), and Intavas	White/orange/dirty white/yellow skin, white/yellow flesh, elongated regular-size, rounded roots, white/dark green, serrated leaves, red tops.	Produces roots even when the plant is old, does not die easily, produces big roots if properly planted, vines produce many roots, weevil-resistant.	Can be stored for one month, takes 4 days to ripen.	Sweet, powdery.	Good for a child who is going to eat his first solid meal, good for camote cue, used as animal feed.

Name	Source	Description	Ripening	Taste	Use
Kawas-was	Don Carlos	Off-white skin, white flesh, regular-sized roots, red leaves.	Roots cluster at the base of plant, vines also produce roots, takes 3–5 months to mature.	Very delicious, sweet, skin peels when cooked.	Good for home consumption.
Kinakaw	Salvacion	Violet skin, yellow flesh, rounded roots.			
Kinampay (Tapol)	Salvacion	Red/white/violet skin, red/violet flesh, small, rounded roots, dark violet leaves.	Produces few roots, takes 3 months to grow.	Sweet, watery/powdery.	Good for home consumption.
Klarin	Salvacion	Red/pink skin, white/yellow flesh, elongated, regular-size/big roots, serrated green leaves.	Does not produce many roots, roots do not cluster in one area, late maturing, takes 3 months to mature and 7 months to produce roots, vines also produce few roots.	Does not ripen. Bland/sweet, not dry/powdery, will not cause colic.	Good for home consumption, used in *benignit*.
Kulating (Kalating)	Intavas, Guilang-guilang, Manolo Fortich (Bukidnon tribe), and Silae, Cabanglasan (Bukidnon tribe)	Yellow/red skin, white/yellow/dark yellow flesh, does not produce big roots, red leaves, red vines, "beautiful" roots.	Produces very few roots, dies easily, sometimes referred to as "joke camote" because it does not give a good harvest.	Ripens in one week, can be stored for one month. Sweet, very powdery, quick-cooking, delicious/good to eat.	Good for home consumption.

Local Varietal[1] Name	Location/Source	Morphological Characteristics	Growth Habit	Postharvest Characteristics	Gastronomic Characteristics	Uses
Kulisok	Silae, Cabanglasan (Bukidnon tribe)	Yellow skin, white flesh, rounded leaves.	Produces many roots.			Good for home consumption, used in *benignit* making.
Kutong	Sungco, Lantapan (Talaandig tribe)	Brown/red skin, violet/white flesh, rounded roots.	Produces few roots.	Does not ripen easily.	Powdery.	Good for home consumption, can be used in ice cream making.
Laguitas	Intavas	Red skin, yellow flesh, small/big, elongated, regular-size roots, serrated/heart-shaped, green leaves.	Dies easily/does not die easily (if the weather is good), produces many roots, takes 5 months to mature.	Takes 4 days to ripen.	Sweet, but not cloying, powdery, can cause colic, not advisable to eat too much of this kind.	
Laguitlit	Salvacion	White skin, yellow/white flesh, small, yellow/light green leaves.	Does not produce many roots.		Sweet/bland watery.	
Lambayong (Gumagatos)	Intavas, Sungco, Lantapan (Talaandig tribe)	White/yellow/orange skin, yellow/orange flesh, roots rounded, big, with no prickly thorns on the surface	Vines also produce roots, can withstand stresses (does not die easily), produces roots at all seasons, produces	Ripens in 3–5 days, can be stored for one month.	Sweet, delicious very powdery, most delicious kind, can cause colic, not advis-	Saleable in the market, good for home consumption, good for *camote cue*

Variety	Source	Description	Roots / maturity	Storage	Taste	Uses
		of the storage roots, small green leaves, red tops.	many roots, takes 4 months to mature.		able to eat too much of this kind.	and *camote* candy, most popular variety in Intavas.
Lampanay	Silae, Cabanglasan (Talaandig tribe)	Brown skin, white flesh, rounded roots.			Leaves are delicious as a vegetable.	Leaves are used as a vegetable.
Lamputi (Inapog)	Silae, Cabanglasan (Bukidnon tribe), Impasug-ong, Malaybalay (Bukidnon tribe), and Intavas	White skin, white flesh, regular-size roots, white, rounded leaves, white vines.	Produces roots even when the plant is old, produces few roots/produces many roots, vines also produce roots, takes 4–5 months to mature.	Can be stored for one month/rots easily, needs one week to ripen/does not ripen.	Sweet/bland, powdery.	Leaves can be used as a vegetable, good for sick people, good for home consumption.
Lawaton	Intavas	White/violet/yellow skin, yellow/mixed-color, violet and yellow flesh.	Produces many roots/produces few roots.		Sweet, very watery.	Good for animal feed, good for *benignit*.
Linggatos (Kabulungan)	Intavas, Sungco, Lantapan (Talaandig tribe)	Yellow skin, yellow flesh, rounded roots, green leaves.	Produces few roots.		Very powdery.	Good for home consumption.
Maasin	Salvacion, Don Carlos	Red/pink skin, white flesh, rounded, elongated roots, red tops.	Takes 6 months to mature, produces more roots at the vines than at the base of the plant, resistant to weevils, hardy.		Very sweet, very powdery.	Good for home consumption, used in fried *camote* and *camote cue*.

Local Varietal[1] Name	Location/ Source	Morphological Characteristics	Growth Habit	Postharvest Characteristics	Gastronomic Characteristics	Uses
Malaga	Sinuda, Kitao-tao (Matigsalog tribe)	Red skin, white flesh, elongated roots, serrated leaves.			Powdery.	
Malanao (Maranao)	Guilang-guilang, Manolo Fortich (Bukidnon tribe)	White/brown skin, white flesh, medium-sized/small, elongated roots, green, serrated, small leaves.	Takes 4 months to mature, vines and base both produce roots.	Takes 3 days to ripen.	Sweet powdery.	Good for sick people, good for home consumption.
Malaybalay	Intavas, Malaybalay	Light violet/pink/red skin, white/yellow flesh, elongated, irregularly shaped roots, white leaves, red tops.	Susceptible to weevils, produces few roots/ produces many roots, vines also produce roots, dies easily.	Roots rot easily.	Not so sweet/ sweet, powdery/not so powdery, quick-cooking.	Good for home consumption.
Malibato	Silae, Cabanglasan (Bukidnon tribe), Kata-blaran, Cabanglasan (Umayamnon tribe), and Sinuda, Kitao-tao (Matigsalog)	Red/black skin, core of flesh is black-and-white, striped yellow flesh, small, rounded, elongated roots like rocks, black leaves.			Delicious, very powdery.	

Manbanwa (Magbanwa)	Salvacion	Red/yellow skin, light yellow flesh, elongated/rounded roots, serrated leaves, red tops.	Roots grow at the base of the plant only, takes 3 months to mature.		Sweet, powdery.	Saleable in the market, good for home consumption.
Mangabay	Sinuda, Kitao-tao (Matigsalog tribe)	Red skin, white flesh.				
Manobo	Intavas	White skin, yellow flesh, rounded green roots.	Good in producing roots.	Ripens easily.	Sweet, powdery.	Good for home consumption.
Manugyang	Intavas	Light violet/yellow/pink/brown skin, pink/yellow flesh, small, straight roots with small prickly roots on the surface of the storage roots.	Produces many roots, takes 6 months to mature.		Watery.	Good for a woman who has just given birth.
Marano	Intavas	Red skin, yellow flesh, rounded roots.	Produces many but small roots, vines also produce roots.		Sweet, powdery.	Good for home consumption.
Masbate	Malaybalay	Red skin, white flesh has "canals" on the surface of the storage roots, serrated, light green leaves.	Does not creep (bushy).		Sweet, powdery.	Used for *camote cue.*

Local Vari-etal[1] Name	Location/ Source	Morphological Characteristics	Growth Habit	Postharvest Characteristics	Gastronomic Characteristics	Uses
Minanaon	Silae, Cabanglasan (Bukidnon tribe)	Red skin, small, rounded roots, small, red leaves.	Produces many roots.		Powdery.	
Natuk (Natok)	Sinuda, Kitao-tao (Matigsalog tribe)	White skin, white flesh, white leaves.			Delicious, powdery.	
Nongnongan	Silae, Cabanglasan (Bukidnon tribe)	Yellow flesh, green leaves.			Powdery.	
Pantawon	Sinuda, Kitao-tao (Matigsalog tribe)	Red skin, white flesh, big, elongated roots.	Roots always come out from the soil, name comes from the property of roots to surface and be seen.			
Pusako	Sinuda, Kitao-tao (Matigsalog tribe)	Red skin, white flesh, roots curvy, straight, and elongated, leaves white and small, some with an itchy-powdery material on the surface.				
Putian	Guilang-guilang, Manolo Fortich (Bukidnon tribe)	White skin, white flesh, white leaves, light green/white vine.			Powdery.	

Name	Location (tribe)	Description	Production	Taste	Use
Puyhad	Katablaran, Cabanglasan (Unayannon tribe)	Reddish brown skin, white flesh.		Powdery.	
Salungag	Silae, Cabanglasan (Bukidnon tribe)	Yellow skin, small, elongated roots, black vines.	Produces many roots.	Delicious.	
Sampalatay	Silae, Cabanglasan (Bukidnon tribe) & Intavas	Red/violet skin, white/yellow flesh, big, rounded, elongated roots, red, rounded leaves.	Produces many roots, vines also produce roots.	Sweet, powdery.	Ripens in one week.
Seventy Days	Salvacion	White/red skin, white flesh, elongated roots, small, green leaves.	Produces few roots, produces roots within 70 days.	Bland/watery.	Animal feed.
Si-uron (Kalugti)	Intavas and Sinuda Kitao-tao (Matigsalog tribe)	Red/violet skin, white flesh, roots irregular-sized, curvy, elongated, and big, green/light green leaves.	Produces many roots, produces roots at the base of the plant, takes 6 months to mature, roots cluster at the base of the plant, dies easily.	Sweet, powdery, does not cause colic.	Can be stored for one month, takes 4 days to ripen. Good for home consumption.
Sidulay (Tidulay)	Dalurong, Kitao-tao (Manobo tribe)	Small roots.			

Local Varietal[1] Name	Location/Source	Morphological Characteristics	Growth Habit	Postharvest Characteristics	Gastronomic Characteristics	Uses
Sikwayon	Silae, Cabanglasan (Bukidnon tribe)	Brown skin, white flesh, serrated leaves.			Sweetens when allowed to ripen, powdery when newly harvested.	
Sil-ipon	Silae, Cabanglasan (Bukidnon tribe), Katablaran (Umayamnon tribe), Intavas, and Salvacion	White/brown skin, white flesh, big, rounded/elongated roots, light green/green leaves.	Produces few roots/produces many roots, both the vines and base produce roots, every node produces roots.	Takes 3 days to ripen.	Very sweet/bland, watery.	Good for home consumption.
Sinig-Yangon	Silae, Cabanglasan (Bukidnon tribe)	White skin, elongated roots, white leaves, has small prickly thorns on the surface of the storage roots.			Powdery	
Subat	Intavas	White/red/pink skin, white/yellow/different-colored flesh, green leaves, violet vines.	Produces few roots (some at the base and a few on the vines), takes 6 months to mature.		Very sweet, not so powdery.	For animal feed, also good for home consumption, can be sold in the market.
Suhuyan	Sinuda, Kitao-tao (Matigsalog tribe)	Curvy roots, flat leaves.	Soil cracks when roots are fully mature.			

Tapol	Salvacion	Violet skin, violet flesh, rounded, heart-shaped roots, red tops, violet vines.	Roots grow at the base of plant, produces many roots.		Sweet, watery/powdery.	Good for home consumption, used for ice candy.
Tidulay (Sidulay)	Katablaran, Cabanglasan (Umayamnon tribe)	Brown skin, white flesh, green leaves.	Produces many roots.		Powdery.	Good for home consumption.
Tinangkong	Intavas and Muntibugao	Red/yellow skin, white flesh; small/big/hardy, regular sized, elongated roots, serrated leaves; two types: one is all-green, the other has red tops.	Can withstand stresses, red type produces more roots than Five-finger while all-green type is not good at producing roots (only 2 to 3 roots/cutting), roots cluster at the base of the plant, 5 months to mature.	Does not ripen/takes 4 days to ripen.	Sweet, delicious/very powdery.	Leaves can be used as a vegetable (especially the tops), good for people who have high blood pressure, good for *camote cue*.
Tinodson (Kayapas, Kinoson)	Intavas	White skin, white flesh, root is big and elongated if produced during full moon, rounded if produced during last quarter of lunar cycle; flat yellow leaves.	Produces many roots at the base of the plant.	Takes 4–7 days to ripen.	Sweet, powdery.	Good for home consumption.
Tuday (Turay)	Salvacion and Intavas	Violet/red/orange skin, white/yellow flesh, small, elongated roots, violet leaves.	Takes 4 months to mature, produces many but small roots.	Takes 3 days to ripen.	Sweet, powdery.	Good for home consumption.

Local Vari- etal[1] Name	Location/ Source	Morphological Characteristics	Growth Habit	Postharvest Characteristics	Gastronomic Characteristics	Uses
Turay (Tuday)	Intavas	Purple/violet/white/ red skin, violet/white, mottled flesh, elon- gated, small roots, white/red serrated leaves, green/red vines.	Produces many roots/ produces few roots, produces roots even during dry season, vines also produce roots but more roots are produced at the base of the plant, takes 5 months to mature.	Ripens in 5 days, rots easily.	Not so sweet/ sweet, not so powdery/ powdery.	Leaves are used as vegetables, good for home consumption, saleable in the market.
Ubihon	Intavas	Violet/red skin, violet flesh, elongated roots, violet, heart-shaped leaves.	Produces many roots/ produces few roots, can withstand stresses (does not die easily), takes 6 months to mature, vines and base of the plant produce roots.	Takes 4 days to ripen.	Bland/sweet, powdery/not powdery.	Good for *benig- nit* (because of the flesh color), used as animal feed.
Valencia	Salvacion and Intavas	Red skin, red/cream/ light yellow/white flesh, rounded/elon- gated, regular sized/ big roots, green flat, big/small, red-edged leaves, red tops.	Produces roots at the base of the plant only, produces many roots, can withstand stresses (does not die easily), will survive if grown in the forest.	Takes one week to ripen.	Not very sweet when newly harvested but sweetens when allowed to ripen, watery/ powdery, can cause colic.	Saleable in the market, too big for broiling, better for boil- ing, good for home consumption.

APPENDIX E

Scientific Evaluations of Indigenous Technologies Associated with Sweet Potato Cultivation in Bukidnon

LAND SELECTION AND PREPARATION

Indigenous Belief or Practice: *Choose dry soil rather than wet soil; the roots will not grow in wet soil.*

> Plant Physiologist 1: Soil should have adequate moisture content for optimum growth of sweet potato—not too dry, not too wet.
>
> Agronomist 1: Dry soil with sufficient moisture is better than wet soil poorly drained.
>
> Agronomist 2: Dry soil probably refers to a sandy soil and the wet soil to clay soil.
>
> Entomologist 1: Planting in wet soil will produce irregular shape of roots, rotting, or no root formation.
>
> Entomologist 2: In dry soil there is sure storage root formation.
>
> Entomologist 3: Roots may rot in waterlogged soil.
>
> Geographer: Excessive soil moisture at planting inhibits tuber initiation.

Indigenous Belief or Practice: *Clearing/cleaning the area is followed by pulverizing the soil.*

> Plant Physiologist 1: Well-cultivated/pulverized soil is essential for optimum sweet potato growth.
>
> Plant Physiologist 2: For easier root establishment.

Note: The same list of indigenous technologies was given for comment to all the scientists included in this sample, but not all scientists gave comments on each item. Only scientists who gave comments on a particular indigenous belief or practice are listed under that category in this appendix.

Agronomist 2: Serves to remove the weeds, facilitate planting, and increase water penetration.

Agronomist 3: Improves aeration and promotes better root growth and storage root development.

Entomologist 1: To enhance establishment of roots.

Entomologist 2: An important agronomic practice.

Entomologist 3: True, practically for all crops.

Geographer: Depends on the soil texture. Heavy clay soil needs to be broken into smaller particles. For lighter soils, this is less important.

Plant Pathologist: When soil is exposed to solar radiation, soil-borne plant pathogens are killed or suppressed. Thus, crops can have a good start and mortality is minimized.

Indigenous Belief or Practice: *Furrowing and hilling-up the soil is done prior to planting.*

Plant Pathologist 1: Done for better root growth.

Plant Pathologist 2: For better root establishment.

Agronomist 2: This is done to facilitate planting and improve aeration.

Entomologist 2: To stabilize plant growth.

Plant Pathologist: Most ideal and scientific.

TIMING

Indigenous Belief or Practice: *Plant when the moon is full because the sea will swell and there will be many shells left on the shore. Hence, sweet potatoes will also have many roots.*

Entomologist 1: This is indicative of planting season.

Entomologist 2: Seems to be associated with the planting season of sweet potato, in rural areas.

Plant Pathologist: Towards the last quarter, there is usually low pressure and rain, and hence more moisture in the soil; plants will readily grow and have a good start.

Indigenous Belief or Practice: *Plant at night when it is very dark so the pests will not attack the plant.*

Entomologist 3: No scientific basis.

Plant Pathologist: Of no significance.

Indigenous Belief or Practice: *Plant in November so there will be as many roots as there are heads in the cemetery during All Souls' Day.*

Entomologist 1: Planting in November is recommended because it is towards the dry season, hence, production of more roots.

Entomologist 2: Good storage root formation during this season.

Entomologist 3: Roots will not be exposed to wet conditions (July–September) which is conducive to rotting and will be ready for harvest at the start of the dry weather in March or April.

SOURCE AND DIVERSITY OF PLANTING MATERIAL

Indigenous Belief or Practice: *Planting materials are given by, or exchanged with, neighbors.*

Plant Physiologist 2: Source does not matter so long as the yield and eating quality are okay.

Agronomist 1: This has undergone prior selection.

Agronomist 2: This needs no explanation.

Entomologist 1: But this is sometimes the source of variety mixtures. Some farmers rename the varieties given to them; it's difficult to trace the original name.

Entomologist 3: These are some of the practices in getting planting materials.

Geographer: As long as these are free of weevil, source is not important.

Indigenous Belief or Practice: *Obtained from other natives across the mountains.*

Plant Physiologist 2: Source does not matter so long as the yield and eating quality are okay.

Agronomist 2: This needs no explanation.

Entomologist 1: But this is sometimes the source of variety mixtures. Some farmers rename the varieties given to them; it's difficult to trace the original name.

Entomologist 3: These are some of the practices in getting planting materials.

Geographer: As long as these are free of weevil, source is not important.

Indigenous Belief or Practice: *Planting more than one variety allows farmers to have a wide range of choices regarding what varieties they feel like eating.*

Agronomist 1: Farmers have a better chance at the market if these are preferred varieties.

Agronomist 2: Different varieties have different eating quality.

Entomologist 3: Yes!

Geographer: Different tubers have different tastes.

Plant Pathologist: Okay!

PLANTING METHODS

Indigenous Belief or Practice: *The hills should be well spaced so there is enough room for roots to grow. Otherwise, the sweet potatoes will just keep producing leaves.*

Plant Physiologist 2: True! Overcrowding means competition for space and nutrients, resulting in smaller roots.

Agronomist 1: We should know the optimum space requirement.

Agronomist 2: It depends on the variety. Long-vined variety needs more space.

Agronomist 3: Minimizes competition for light and nutrients.

Entomologist 1: Wider spacing produces bigger roots but fewer number of roots.

Entomologist 2: Plant spacing is very important in the formation of acceptable storage root size.

Entomologist 3: Not sure.

Geographer: Plant density is not very important for total tuber yield. But spacing does influence the tuber size. Closer spacing gives more but smaller tubers.

Plant Pathologist: Sound.

Indigenous Belief or Practice: *Bite the vines before planting so a lot of roots will be produced.*

Entomologist 3: No scientific basis.

Plant Pathologist: Purely fanatic.

Indigenous Belief or Practice: *Planting is done by kneeling and covering each newly planted hill with all ten fingers so the cuttings will produce as many roots.*

Entomologist 3: No scientific basis.

Plant Pathologist: Purely fanatic.

Indigenous Belief or Practice: *Thorns of cogon grass and rattan are mixed with planting materials to induce the formation of many roots and to make the roots cluster in one area, respectively.*

Entomologist 3: No scientific basis.

Plant Pathologist: Of no significance.

MATERIALS MIXED WITH CUTTINGS

Indigenous Belief or Practice: *Ginger and peanuts are mixed with planting materials for weevil resistance, and for good harvest, respectively.*

Agronomist 1: Probably ginger has some repellant action on weevil.

Agronomist 3: Repellant properties of both crops have not been studied, but they may have been observed by farmers.

Entomologist 1: Since peanut can fix nitrogen through rhizobial action, it can increase yield, but intercropping is not recommended (perhaps sweet potato after peanut). Ginger acts as repellant.

Entomologist 2: Ginger may act as repellant for weevil.

Entomologist 3: No scientific basis.

Geographer: Ginger may repel sweet potato weevil.

Plant Pathologist: Ginger may be weevil repellant, and intercropping is one method of pest control.

Indigenous Belief or Practice: *Holy water is mixed with some cuttings so God will watch over and protect the crops.*

Entomologist 3: Hard to prove.
Plant Pathologist: Purely fanatic.

SEXUAL DIVISION OF LABOR

Indigenous Belief or Practice: *Elderly females should be the ones to plant since they are more familiar with traditional beliefs and practices.*

Agronomist 2: In their society, the elderly females probably have more experience.
Entomologist 1: Perhaps they are already experts.
Entomologist 3: No, just teach the young ones regarding sound practices.
Plant Pathologist: Purely fanatic.

Indigenous Belief or Practice: *Females should plant since it is an easy job and the sweet potato plot is near the house.*

Entomologist 3: Whoever has the time.
Plant Pathologist: Purely fanatic.

Indigenous Belief or Practice: *Males should plant since females do the household chores.*

Agronomist 2: If females are occupied with other tasks, then it will have to be the males who will plant.
Entomologist 3: Whoever is more free to do the work.

CULTURAL MANAGEMENT

Indigenous Belief or Practice: *Creeping vines should be covered with soil so these will produce roots.*

Plant Physiologist 1: To increase yield.
Plant Physiologist 2: True!
Agronomist 1: There are varieties that produce marketable roots in the creeping vines.
Agronomist 2: The purpose of covering is to allow the roots to develop into storage roots.
Agronomist 3: Covered internodes generally produce storage roots.
Entomologist 1: Vines are used as planting materials, therefore covering them with soil will initiate root formation.
Entomologist 3: Only if staggered harvesting is desired, usually for home use. Roots pro-

duced on secondary branches will be ready for harvest later than those at the main stem. Geographer: They will produce tubers, but it is probably dependent on the variety. Not very important.

Indigenous Belief or Practice: *Grasses and weeds are cut using a scythe* (sanggot) *or long-bladed knife* (bolo) *to maintain cleanliness of the area.*

Plant Physiologist 1: If the farmer has enough resources to clean the area, he can clean the area. If not, the crop will not be adversely affected.

Agronomist 1: Clean culture is important, and farmers use *bolo* for weeding.

Agronomist 2: This minimizes competition for light, nutrients, and water.

Agronomist 3: Spot weeding is important, especially in crops that are more than two months old.

Entomologist 1: Weeds compete for light, nutrients, and water.

Entomologist 2: To minimize plant-weed competition.

Entomologist 3: To improve plant growth.

Plant Pathologist: Sound.

Indigenous Belief or Practice: *Weeding is done only once for the entire planting season.*

Agronomist 2: Frequency depends on the weed population, but as an average once a year is okay.

Entomologist 2: Depends on the persistence of the weeds while sweet potato is still in the vegetative stage.

Entomologist 3: Depending on how fast the canopy cover is formed.

Geographer: Sweet potato does not need a lot of weeding.

Indigenous Belief or Practice: *Rats are left to eat as much as they can since they cannot eat everything anyway.*

Agronomist 2: Chemical control of pests is also expensive and dangerous.

Plant Pathologist: Sweet potato is a low-income crop, so use of pesticide will just increase cost of production and reduce return on investment.

Indigenous Belief or Practice: *Allow insects and other pests to eat as much as they can eat because if they are "touched" they will become more angry and will damage everything in the field.*

Entomologist 1: "Allow insects" because some of them act as biological control agents.

Entomologist 2: A natural pest control measure.

Entomologist 3: No!

Plant Pathologist: Nonsense!

Indigenous Belief or Practice: *Completely cover the roots with soil to prevent the weevil from damaging them.*

Plant Physiologist 1: Hilling-up is an effective means of controlling weevil damage.

Agronomist 1: Exposed roots are easily attacked by weevil.

Agronomist 2: Exposed roots are more susceptible to weevil attack.

Entomologist 1: Exposing the roots provides an access to weevil. Hilling up is done to avoid weevil infestation. Soil cracking is also minimized.

Entomologist 2: Cultural practice.

Entomologist 3: This will help. The soil layer on top of the roots can serve as mechanical barrier to weevil penetration.

Geographer: This makes it more difficult for weevils to attack tubers.

Plant Pathologist: Sound!

HARVESTING METHODS

Indigenous Belief or Practice: *Stick or sharpened wood instead of a knife* (lub-ang *or* kali) *is used for harvesting so that vines and smaller roots won't be damaged.*

Plant Physiologist 1: Wooden sticks are not enough for harvesting.

Agronomist 1: Most farmers are using this technique.

Agronomist 2: The bigger the tool, the greater the chance of injuring roots.

Agronomist 3: Applicable to smaller area or sloping areas.

Entomologist 1: Injury will be an entry point of disease infection.

Entomologist 3: Appropriate only in light or loose soil. Wood will not inflict damage on the roots and vines as readily as a *bolo* or knife would.

Plant Pathologist: Okay!

Indigenous Belief or Practice: *Harvest only the big roots as needed and leave the smaller ones to grow in the field. This way, sweet potatoes will continue producing roots.*

Plant Physiologist 1: Appropriate for subsistence farming.

Plant Physiologist 2: Right!

Agronomist 1: This is done to have a stable supply of sweet potato in the market.

Agronomist 2: Sweet potato is a perennial, and it will continue to grow as long as it is still alive.

Entomologist 2: Priming increases marketable yield.

Entomologist 3: Depends on the variety, rainfall, and purpose. If for home consumption, staggered harvesting is advantageous. But new shoots may be produced continuously by some varieties if soil moisture is always available.

Geographer: A useful technique for spreading the yield over a longer period of time.

Plant Pathologist: Common practice.

Indigenous Belief or Practice: *Harvest on time (i.e., 4 months after planting) so that the roots will not rot.*

Plant Physiologist 1: This is usual practice of sweet potato growers.

Agronomist 1: Specially if you suspect tuber rot disease.

Agronomist 2: Most varieties mature in four months.

Entomologist 1: Depends on variety/maturity of the plant and time of planting. During rainy season, a longer period towards maturity is required.

Entomologist 2: Roots will rot only if planting during or towards the wet season.

Entomologist 3: Yes or no, depending on the variety (i.e., if all roots mature at the same time). Sprouting of roots may occur if big roots are not harvested after the vines die.

Geographer: Sweet potato tubers can be left for some time in the soil, but not for long.

Plant Pathologist: Crop is fully matured and dry matter content is high.

Indigenous Belief or Practice: *Never allow the male to do the harvesting or he will thereafter behave like a wild boar.*

Entomologist 3: No!

Geographer: No, I do not think so.

Plant Pathologist: No scientific significance.

Indigenous Belief or Practice: *Female does the harvesting because it is an easy job.*

Plant Physiologist 1: Either male or female can do the harvesting.

Entomologist 3: Only if male is engaged in other productive work.

Plant Pathologist: No scientific significance.

Indigenous Belief or Practice: *Males harvest and eat the first three roots. This way, the rest of the roots become dry and powdery.*

Entomologist 3: No scientific basis.

Geographer: There are no doubt sound reasons for this division of labor, but not agronomic reasons.

Plant Pathologist: Not significant.

Indigenous Belief or Practice: *By staggering the harvest, roots are stored underground until they are needed.*

Plant Physiologist 2: True!

Agronomist 1: Natural storage.

Agronomist 2: Very logical.

Agronomist 3: Applicable especially in areas where sweet potato is staple or supplement to rice or corn.

Entomologist 1: Underground storage increases sugar content.

Entomologist 3: Yes, up to a certain point. The roots may sprout later.

Plant Pathologist: This kind of storage should be only for a definite period of time. Sweet potato tubers will become cottony if stored underground for too long.

POST-HARVEST METHODS

Indigenous Belief or Practice: *Do not wash the roots that will be stored because the skin will dry up and break when exposed to the sun.*

Plant Physiologist 2: Incomplete drying will cause microbial infestation and rotting.

Agronomist 1: Air dry only.

Agronomist 2: Washing facilitates rotting as the skin is damaged and rotting organisms penetrate the flesh.

Entomologist 3: There may be bruising during the washing process, and this will be an entry point for pathogenic microorganisms.

Geographer: If stored wet, tubers may rot.

Plant Pathologist: Increasing the moisture on the skin exposes the roots to favorable conditions for disease infection.

Nutritionist: Partly true. There is faster evaporation of moisture with clean skin, but there will be shriveling upon drying rather than breaking of skin.

Indigenous Belief or Practice: *"Excess" roots are placed in an underground pit lined with leaves, cellophane, or sack and topped with a layer of soil.*

Plant Physiologist 1: Cellophane may not be good for storing sweet potato.

Plant Physiologist 2: Storage practice.

Agronomist 1: Underground storage system.

Agronomist 2: This is one method of storage. This stimulates the condition of the roots when still attached to the plant.

Entomologist 1: "Pile system" to avoid injury of roots.

Entomologist 2: Post-harvest practice.

Entomologist 3: This may be practical for farmers, but it is better to keep roots in well-ventilated areas where dampness conducive to rotting can be avoided.

Plant Pathologist: These methodologies on storage are sound and practical depending on the situation existing in the area.

Indigenous Belief or Practice: *"Excess" roots are sliced into smaller pieces and dried in the sun. Dried chips can last for months.*

Plant Physiologist 2: True!

Agronomist 1: One aspect of processing.

Agronomist 2: A very good way of preservation.

Entomologist 2: Post-harvest practice.

Entomologist 3: This is done by some subsistence farmers to prolong storage life.

Nutritionist: Low moisture content and closed containers contribute to longer shelf life.

UTILIZATION

Indigenous Belief or Practice: *Sweet potato roots can be used as a staple in the absence of rice or corn or as a side dish in the absence of meat or fish.*

Plant Physiologist 2: Depends on the individual.

Agronomist 1: Roots can be used as vegetable with coconut milk.

Agronomist 2: Very good energy source, although lacking in protein.

Entomologist 3: The fleshy roots are rich in carbohydrates, but not a good source of protein.

Plant Pathologist: Okay!

Nutritionist: Partly yes. It is an energy-giving food like cereal but cannot substitute for fish or meat as a protein source.

Indigenous Belief or Practice: *Leaves are used to heal skin diseases such as* kugab *and to relieve itchy skin.*

Plant Physiologist 1: Not sure.

Plant Physiologist 2: Without clinical proof, as far as I know.

Agronomist 1: Some of the old folks are using this.

Agronomist 3: No scientific studies have been done on this aspect, but we cannot understand experience. Their use for curing specific diseases could have been practiced in the past and may have proven effective.

Entomologist 2: Of medicinal value.

Entomologist 3: Not knowledgeable on this aspect.

Geographer: Not sure.

Plant Pathologist: The medicinal uses of sweet potato leaves and tubers have long been resorted to in the rural areas.

NOTES

CHAPTER 1. OF MEMORIES AND VARIETIES

1. *Diversity*, or more precisely, biotic diversity, is here defined as the extent of variability or the number of different kinds of life forms. It occurs at the interspecific or community level (e.g., different plants, animals, and microorganisms constituting a forest ecosystem or different insects and crops in a farmer's field) and at the intraspecific or varietal level. *Genetic diversity* refers to the variability of the gene pool of a particular species—or intraspecific diversity—and is the focus of discussion of the present work.

2. The term *landraces*, or folk varieties, refers to types of plant genetic resources that have evolved as a result of indigenous selection and breeding and, in most cases, that are propagated under traditional farming systems (in contrast, for example, to modern high-yielding varieties). Many of the local sweet potato varieties documented in this study fall into this category.

3. Accessions are living samples of biological specimens held in gene banks, and their number usually run to thousands. Each plant, animal, or microorganism sample to be included in the gene bank is given an accession number upon acquisition, and any information pertaining to that particular holding can be retrieved through its accession number.

CHAPTER 3. MODERNIZATION AND THE DISTRIBUTION OF INDIGENOUS KNOWLEDGE

1. A *sitio* is a second-level politico-geographical unit in the Philippines. It is composed of a few to several contiguous *baranggays*, the basic political unit in the Phillipines (see note 1, chapter 5).

2. A *carabao*, or water buffalo, is traditionally used to pull the plow during land preparation. Because of this role, it has often been referred to as "the beast of burden."

3. A "can" (used as a measure for buying and selling produce like rice, corn, and sweet potato) is roughly equivalent to 14 liters.

4. Farming is considered a performance because it follows a script that is in the minds of local farmers. Within limits, this script is socially shared and culturally transmitted. Someone who has no knowledge of the order of activities and decisions to be made, for example, obviously cannot be a very effective or productive farmer.

CHAPTER 6. CULTURAL ALTERNATIVES IN GERMPLASM CONSERVATION

1. A *baranggay* is the basic political structure in the Philippine government system. It is headed by a local *baranggay* captain, who answers to the villagers below and the town mayor above.

2. UPWARD is an acronym for the User's Perspective with Agricultural Research and Development. The name is also suggestive of generating technologies and validating knowledge from the ground up instead of the other way around. In many respects, it is geared towards the reversal of the top-down approach so prevalent in the development strategies of the 1960s and the 1970s in which agricultural technologies were generated in land grant universities and international research centers and extended to farmers in developing countries.

LITERATURE CITED

Alcorn, Janice B. 1984. *Huastec Mayan Ethnobotany*. Austin: University of Texas Press.

Alcorn, Janice B., and C. Hernandez. 1983. Plants of the Huastec Region of Mexico with Analysis of their Huastec Names. *Journal of Mayan Linguistics* 4:11–118.

Altieri, Miguel A., and Laura C. Merrick. 1987. Agroecology and *In Situ* Conservation of Native Crop Diversity in the Third World. In *BioDiversity*, ed. E. O. Wilson. Washington, D.C.: National Academy Press.

Altieri, Miguel A., A. van Schoonhoven, and J. D. Doll. 1977. The Ecological Role of Weeds in Insect Pest Management Systems: A Review Associated with Bean (*Phaseolus vulgaris* L.) Cropping Systems. *Pest Articles News and Summ.* (PANS) 23:195–205.

Annikster, Y. 1988. The Biological Structure of Native Populations of Wild Emmer Wheat in Israel. *Final Report to USDA (ARS)*. Oregon State University and the National Council for Research and Development, Israel.

Avise, John. 1994. *Molecular Markers, Natural History, and Evolution*. New York: Chapman and Hall.

Bejema, C. J. 1972. Transmission of Information about the Environment in the Human Species. *Social Biology* 19:224–226.

Bentley, Jeffrey, and K. L. Andrew. 1991. Pests, Peasants, and Publications: Anthropological and Entomological Views of an Integrated Pest Management Program for Small-Scale Honduran Farmers. *Human Organization* 50(2):113–124.

Berland, Joseph. 1982. *No Five Fingers are Alike: Cognitive Amplifiers in Social Context*. Cambridge: Harvard University Press.

Berlin, Brent. 1970. *A Preliminary Ethnobotanical Survey of the Auguaruna Region of the*

Upper Marañon River Valley, Amazonas, Peru. Washington D.C.: Report to Wenner-Gren Foundation for Anthropological Research.

Borgatti, Stephen. 1996. *Anthropac 4.0 User's Guide.* Natick, Mass.: Analytic Technologies.

Boster, James. 1984. Classification, Cultivation, and Selection of Aguaruna Cultivars of *Manihot esculenta* (Eurpherbiaceae). *Advances in Economic Botany* 1:34–47.

———. 1986. Requiem for the Omniscient Informant: There's Life in the Old Girl Yet. In *Directions in Cognitive Anthropology*, ed. J. Dougherty. Urbana: University of Illinois Press.

Brokensha, D., D. M. Warren, and O. Werner, eds. 1982. *Indigenous Knowledge Systems and Development.* Washington, D.C.: University Press of America.

Brush, Stephen. 1990. Crop Development in Centers of Domestication: A Case Study of Andean Potato Agriculture. In *Agroecology and Small-Farm Development*, ed. M. Altieri and S. Hecht. Boca Raton: CRC Press.

———. 1991. A Farmer-Based Approach to Conserving Crop Germplasm. *Economic Botany* 45:153–165.

———. 1992. Reconsidering the Green Revolution: Diversity and Stability in Cradle Areas of Crop Domestication. *Human Ecology* 20(2):145–167.

Busch, Lawrence. 1993. Ethical and Social Issues of Protection in Intellectual Property Rights. In *Intellectual Property Rights: Protection of Plant Materials*, ed. S. Baenzigger, et al. CSSA Special Publication No. 21. Madison, Wis.: Crop Science Society of America.

Buttell, Frederick. 1993. Ideology and Agricultural Technology in the Late Twentieth Century: Biotechnology as Symbol and Substance. *Agriculture and Human Values.* Spring:5–15.

Chacon, J. C., and Stephen Gleissman. 1982. Use of the "Non-weed" Concept in Traditional Tropical Agro-ecosystems of Southeastern Mexico. *Ecosystems* 8:1–11.

Chambers, Robert. 1990a. Farmer First: A Practical Paradigm for Third World Agriculture. In *Agroecology and Small-Farm Development*, ed. M. Altieri and S. Hecht. Boca Raton: CRC Press.

———. 1990b. *Microenvironments Unobserved.* International Institute for Environmental and Development Gatekeeper Series No. 22:1–18. London: Sustainable Agriculture Programme, IIED.

Chujoy, Enrique. 1990. International Potato Center (personal communication).

Clawson, David. 1985. Harvest Security and Intraspecific Diversity in Traditional Tropical Agriculture. *Economic Botany* 39:56–67.

Cleveland, D. A., and D. Soleri. 1987. Household Gardens as a Development Strategy. *Human Organization* 46(3):259–270.

Cole, Fay Cooper. 1956. *The Bukidnon of Mindanao.* In *Fieldiana: Anthropology.* Chicago: Chicago Natural History Museum.

Conklin, Harold. 1954. *An Ethnoecological Approach to Shifting Agriculture*. Transactions of the New York Academy of Sciences, Series II, 17:133–142.

Dempsey, Gerard J. 1992. Diversity and Crop Defence: The Role of Farmer and Breeder. *Biotechnology and Development Monitor* 13:13–15.

Deshmukh, Ian. 1989. On the Limited Role of Biologists in Biological Conservation. *Diversity* 3(3):321.

Edgerton, Ronald K. 1979. Frontier Society on the Bukidnon Plateau: 1870–1941. In *Global Trade and Local Transformations*, ed. Alfred W. McCoy and Ed C. de Jesus. ASAA: Southeast Asia Publication Series.

Food and Agriculture Organization (FAO). 1989. Report to the Commission on Plant Genetic Resources, Rome.

Fowler, Cary, and Roy Pat Mooney. 1990. *Shattering: Food, Politics, and Loss of Genetic Diversity*. Tucson: University of Arizona Press.

Fujisaka, Samuel. 1988. Incorporating Farmer Knowledge in International Rice Research. Paper for CIP Rockfeller Foundation Conference on Farmers and Food Systems (September 26–30, 1988), Lima, Peru.

———. 1992. Farmer Knowledge and Sustainability in Rice-Farming Systems: Blending Science and Indigenous Innovation. In *Diversity, Farmer Knowledge, and Sustainability*, ed. J. L. Moock and R. E. Rhoades. Ithaca, N.Y.: Cornell University Press.

Gladwin, Christina. 1980. A Theory of Real-Life Choice: Applications to Agricultural Decision Making. In *Agricultural Decision Making: Anthropological Contributions to Rural Development*, ed. P. E. Barlett. New York: Academic Press.

Hawkes, Jack G. 1991. The Importance of Genetic Resources in Plant Breeding. *Biological Journal of the Linnean Society* 43(1):3–10.

Herskovitz, Annette. 1986. *Language and Spatial Cognition*. Cambridge: Cambridge University Press.

Heywood, Vernon H. 1990. Taxonomy, Biosystematics, and Conservation. In *Conservation Biology: A Training Manual for Biological Diversity and Genetic Resources*, ed. P. Kapoor-Vijay and J. White. London: Commonwealth Secretariat.

Hodgkin, T., and Ramanatha Raov. 1992. IBPGR and the Conservation of Landraces. Discussion Paper. Rome: IBPGR.

Holden, John, James Peacock, and Trevor Williams. 1993. *Genes, Crops, and the Environment*. Cambridge and New York: Cambridge University Press.

Huaman, Zosimo. 1988. Current Status of the Maintenance of Sweet Potato Genetic Resources at CIP. In *Exploration, Maintenance, and Utilization of Sweet Potato Genetic Resources*. Report of the Sweet Potato Planning Conference. Lima: International Potato Center.

Huaman, Zosimo, and Peter Scheneidiche. 1991. The Importance of *Ex Situ* Conservation of Germplasm. *Diversity* 7(1–2):68–69.

Hunn, Eugene. 1985. The Utilitarian in Folk Biological Classification. In *Directions in Cognitive Anthropology*, ed. J. Dougherty. Urbana: University of Illinois Press.

Ingram, G. Brent. 1990. Management of Biosphere Reserves for the Conservation and Utilization of Genetic Resources: The Social Choices. *Impact of Science on Society* 40(2):123–141.

International Board for Plant Genetic Resources. 1989. *Annual Report, 1988*. Rome: IBPGR.

Jackson, Michael, and Huggan, Robert. 1991. Sharing the Diversity of Rice to Feed the World. *Diversity* 9(3):23–25.

Jiggins, Janice. 1986. *Gender-Related Impacts and the Work of the International Agricultural Research Centers*. Washington, D.C.: World Bank.

Johannsen, Agneta. 1992. Applied Anthropology and Postmodernist Ethnography. *Human Organization* 5(1):71–81.

Jondle, Robert. 1989. Overview and Status of Plant Proprietary Rights. In *Intellectual Property Rights Associated with Plants*. Madison, Wis.: Crop Science Society of America, American Society of Agronomy, and Soil Science Society of America.

Keesing, Roger M. 1987. Models, Folk and Cultural: Paradigm Regained? In *Cultural Models in Language and Thought*, ed. D. Holland and N. Quinn. Cambridge and New York: Cambridge University Press.

Keystone Center. 1991. *Final Consensus Report of the Keystone International Dialogue Series on Plant Genetic Resources, Madras Plenary Session*. Keystone, Colo.: Keystone Center.

King, F. H. 1927. *Farmers of Forty Centuries: Or, Permanent Agriculture in China, Korea and Japan*. New York: Harcourt and Brace.

Kloppenburg, Jack R. 1990. No Hunting: Scientific Poaching and Global Biodiversity. *Z Magazine* September, 104–108.

Knight, C. Gregory, 1980. Ethnoscience and African Farmers: Rationale and Strategy. In *Indigenous Knowledge Systems and Development*, ed. D. W. Brokensha and D. M. Warren. Boston: University Press of America.

Kosko, Bart. 1993. *Fuzzy Thinking: The New Science of Fuzzy Logic*. New York: Hyperion.

Lacy, William B. 1995. The Global Plant Genetic Resources System: A Competition-Cooperation Paradox. *Crop Science* 35(2):335–345.

Levi-Strauss, Claude. 1966. *The Savage Mind*. Chicago: University of Chicago Press.

Lightfoot, Clive. 1987. Indigenous Research and On-Farm Trials. *Agricultural Administration and Extension* 24:79–89.

Lightfoot, Clive, Roque de Pedro, and Florencio Saladaga. 1987. Screening Sweet Potato Cultivars by Subsistence Farmers: Implications for Breeding. Paper presented during the International Root Crops Symposium (May 23–30), Leyte, Philippines.

Lipton, Michael. 1989. *New Seeds and Poor People*. London: Unwin Hyman.

McNabb, Steven. 1991. The Uses of "Inaccurate Data": A Methodological Critique and Application of Alaska Native Data. *American Anthropologist* 92:116–129.

Mooney, Pat Roy. 1993. Exploiting Local Knowledge: International Policy Implications. In *Cultivating Knowledge*, ed. Walter de Boef, K. Amanor, and K. Wellard. London: Intermediate Technology Publications.

Nabhan, Gary P. 1986. Native American Crop Diversity, Genetic Resource Conservation and the Policy of Neglect. *Agriculture and Human Values* 2:14–17.

Nabhan, Gary P., Donna House, Suzan A. Humberto, Wendy Hodson, Luis Hernandez, and Guadalupe Malda. 1991. Conservation and Use of Rare Plants by Traditional Cultures of the U.S./Mexico Borderlands. In *Biodiversity: Culture, Conservation, and Ecodevelopment*, ed. Margery M. Oldfield and Janice Alcorn. Boulder, Colo.: Westview Press.

National Research Council. 1992. *Conserving Biodiversity: A Research Agenda for Development Agencies*. Washington D.C.: National Academy Press.

Nazarea-Sandoval, Virginia. 1990. Memory Banking of Indigenous Technologies of Local Farmers Associated with Traditional Crop Varieties: A Focus on Sweet Potato. *Proceedings of the Inaugural Workshop on the User's Perspective with Agricultural Research and Development*. Los Banos: UPWARD/International.

———. 1992. Ethnoagronomy and Ethnogastronomy: On Indigenous Typology and Use of Biological Resources. *Agriculture and Human Values* 8:121–131.

———. 1995. *Local Knowledge and Agricultural Decision Making in the Philippines: Class, Gender, and Resistance*. Ithaca, N.Y.: Cornell University Press.

Nazarea, Virginia D., Eleanor Tison, Maricel C. Piniero, and Robert E. Rhoades. 1997. *Yesterday's Ways, Tomorrow's Treasures: Heirloom Plants and Memory Banking*. Dubuque, Ia.: Kendall/Hunt Publishing Company.

Oldfield, Margaret, and Janice Alcorn. 1991. Conservation of Traditional Agroecosystems. In *Biodiversity, Culture, Conservation and Ecodevelopment*, ed. M. L. Oldfield and J. B. Alcorn. Boulder, Colo.: Westview Press.

Paddock, Christine, and Wil deJong. 1991. The House Gardens of Santa Rosa: Diversity and Variability in an Amazonian Agricultural System. *Economic Botany* 42(2):166–175.

Palmberg, Christel, and J. T. Esquinas-Alcazar. 1990. The Role of the United Nations Agencies and Other International Organizations in the Conservation of Plant Genetic Resources. *Forest Ecology and Management* 35:171–197.

Piniero, Maricel. 1991. Comparative Study of Sweet Potato Production System Relative to Degree of Commercialization: The Case of Intavas and Salvacion. In *Sweet Potato Cultures of Asia and South Pacific*, ed. R. E. Rhoades and V. N. Sandoval. Proceedings of the Second Annual International Conference. Los Banos: User's Perspective with Agricultural Research and Development.

Plucknett, D. L., et al. 1987. *Gene Banks and the World's Food*. Princeton, N.J.: Princeton University Press.

Prain, Gordon, and Maricel Piniero. 1994. Community Curatorship of Plant Genetic Resources in Southern Philippines: Preliminary Findings. In *Local Knowledge,*

Global Knowledge, and Plant Genetic Resources: Towards a Partnership, ed. G. Prain and C. P. Bagalonon. Los Banos: User's Perspective with Agricultural Research and Development.

Quiros, C. F., et al. 1990. Biochemical and Folk Assessment of Variability of Andean Cultivated Potatoes. *Economical Botany* 44:245–266.

Rappaport, Roy. 1968. *Pigs for the Ancestors*. New Haven: Yale University Press.

Raymond, Ruth. 1993. Conserving Nature's Biodiversity: The Role of the International Plant Genetic Resources Institute. *Diversity* 9(3):254–266.

Rhoades, Robert. 1990. The Coming Revolution for Rural Development Research. In *Asian Training of Trainers on Farm Household Diagnostic Skills*, ed. R. E. Rhoades, V. N. Sandoval, and C. P. Bagalonon. Los Banos: User's Perspective with Agricultural Research and Development.

———. 1990. International Potato Center/User's Perspective with Agricultural Research and Development (personal communication).

———. 1994. Indigenous People and the Preservation of Biodiversity. *Hortscience* 29(11):1222–1225.

Rhoades, Robert E., and R. Booth. 1982. Farmer-Back-to-Farmer. *Agricultural Administration* 11:127–137.

Rhoades, Robert E., and Anthony Bebbington. 1995. Farmers Who Experiment: An Untapped Resource for Agricultural Research and Development. In *Indigenous Knowledge Systems: The Cultural Dimension of Development*, ed. P. M. Warren, D. Brokensha, and L. J. Slikkerveer. London: Intermediate Technology Publications.

Richards, Paul. 1985. *Indigenous Agricultural Revolution: Ecology and Food Production in West Africa*. Boulder, Colo.: Westview Press.

Rick, Charles M. 1958. The Role of Natural Hybridization in the Derivation of Cultivated Tomatoes of Western South America. *Economic Botany* 12:346–367.

Romney, Kimball, S. C. Weller, and W. H. Batchelder. 1986. Culture as Consensus: A Theory of Culture and Informant Accuracy. *American Anthropologist* 88:313–338.

Rosch, Eleanor. 1978. Principles of Categorization. In *Cognition and Categorization*, ed. E. Rosch and B. B. Lloyd. Hillsdale, N.J.: Erlbaum.

Sachs, Carolyn. 1992. Reconsidering Diversity in Agriculture and Food Systems: An Ecofeminist Approach. *Agriculture and Human Values* 9(3):4–10.

Scott, James. 1990. *Domination and the Arts of Resistance: Hidden Transcripts*. New Haven, Conn.: Yale University Press.

Sealy, Nicholas J. 1993. Intellectual Property Rights in Plants. In *Intellectual Property Rights: Protection of Plant Materials*, ed. S. Baenzigger et al. CSSA Special Publication No. 21. Madison, Wis.: Crop Science Society of America.

Shiva, Vandana. 1993. *Monoculture of the Mind: Perspectives on Biodiversity and Biotechnology*. London and Penang: Zed Books.

————. 1993. Women's Indigenous Knowledge and Biodiversity Conservation. In *Eco-feminism*, ed. M. Mies and V. Shiva. Halifax and London: Fernwood Press.

Soleri, Daniela, and David Cleveland. 1993. Hopi Crop Diversity and Change. *Journal of Ethnobiology* 13(2):203–231.

Sperling, Louise. 1992. Farmer Participation and the Development of Bean Varieties in Rwanda. In *Diversity, Farmer Knowledge, and Sustainability*, ed. J. L. Moock and R. E. Rhoades. Ithaca, N.Y.: Cornell University Press.

Tversky, Amos. 1972. Eliminational by Aspects: A Theory of Choice. *Psychology Review* (4):281–291.

Van Dorp, Marianne, and Tom Rulkens. 1993. Farmer Crop-Selection Criteria and Gene Bank Collections in Indonesia. In *Cultivating Knowledge*, ed. W. de Boef, K. Amanor, and K. Wellard. London: Intermediate Technology Publications.

Van Oosterhout, Saskia. 1993. Sorghum Genetic Resources of Small-Scale Farmers in Zimbabwe. In *Cultivating Knowledge*, ed. W. de Boef, K. Amanor, and K. Wellard. London: Intermediate Technology Publications.

Van Soest, Louis J. M. 1990. Plant Genetic Resources: Safe for the Future in Gene Banks. *Impact of Science on Society* 158:107–120.

Vaughn, Duncan. 1988. International Rice Germplasm Center, International Rice Research Institute (personal communication).

Warren, Michael. 1984. Linking Scientific and Indigenous Systems. In *The Transformation of International Agricultural Research and Development*, ed. J. L. Compton. Boulder, Colo.: Westview Press.

Wilkes, G. 1984. Germplasm Conservation toward the Year 2000. In *Plant Genetic Resources: A Conservation Imperative*, ed. C. W. Yeatman, D. Kafton, and G. Wilkes. Boulder, Colo.: Westview Press.

World Resources Institute (WRI), World Conservation Union (IUCN), and United Nations Environment Programme (UNEP). 1992. *Global Biodiversity Strategy: Guidelines for Action to Save, Study, and Use the Earth's Biotic Wealth Sustainably and Equitably*.

Zimmerer, Karl S., and David S. Douches. 1991. Geographical Approaches to Native Crop Research and Conservation: The Partitioning of Genetic Diversity in Andean Potatoes. *Economic Botany* 45:176–189.

INDEX

Mindanao, 37, 38(fig.), 76
Mindoro, 2
modernization, 2, 35
monoculture, 6–7, 9
Mooney, Roy Pat, 116–17
Mother's Craft, 99

National Research Council: *Conserving Biodiversity*, 35
nature, 80–81
networking: and gene banking, 99–102
New People's Army (NPA), 42

patents, 116
Peacock, James, 92
pest control, 54–55, 61, 64, 76–77, 78, 83, 105, 170–71
Philippines, 2, 4, 175n. 1, 176n. 1; rice crops in, 9, 87; sweet potatoes in, 12, 90
plant breeders' rights, 118
planting: methods of, 78, 82, 85, 105, 167–69; timing of, 61, 76, 166–67
Plant Patent Act (1930), 116
Plant Variety Protection Act (PVPA), 119
potatoes, 4
Prain, Gordon, 108
preliminary participant observation, 23–25
Putihon, 40
PVPA. *See* Plant Variety Protection Act

rainy season, 61
rapid appraisal, 23–25
rapid rural appraisal (RRA), 23
reconstruction: diagramming from memory, 29–31; and gatekeepers, 26–27; life history and, 27–29
rice, 9, 87
root crops, 19, 102(table); in Dalwangan, 96, 98(table), 106–8; in Intavas, 39, 40
RRA. *See* rapid rural appraisal
Rwanda, 87

Sachs, Carolyn, 113
Salvacion, 37, 38(fig.); agriculture in, 40–41, 42–43; commercialization in, 41–42; crop varieties in, 45(table), 46, 74, 77, 143; cultivation practices in, 60–61, 76–77, 84–86, 104–6, 122–40; indigenous knowledge in, 58, 86; varietal selection in, 52, 66–68
Sawaga River, 95
scientists, science: and indigenous technologies, 53–58
scripts, 53–54
SECA. *See* Socioeconomic and Cultural Aspects
settlements, 23
Shiva, Vandana, 88, 115
Sil-ipon, 40
Socioeconomic and Cultural Aspects (SECA), 11
socioeconomic survey, 141–42
sorting and ranking, 32–33
Sumbawa, 49
sweet potatoes: as cash crop, 42–43; cultivation practices and, 60–64, 81–86, 104–6, 122–40; ideal variety of, 71–72; indigenous knowledge of, 56–57(table); indigenous technology and, 165–74; in life histories, 28–29; local description of, 64–66; local technologies and, 36–37; in Philippines, 4, 12–13, 90; triad tests on, 46–49; varietal selection of, 50(table), 51–53, 66–68, 83, 84–85; varieties of, 45(table), 46, 75, 76, 77–78, 86–87, 106, 146–64
symbolism, 80–81
systematization: processes of, 31–34

Tarlac Agricultural College (TAC), 90
technology, 6, 8, 14, 74–75, 79, 176n. 2; indigenous, 165–74; in Intavas, 39–40; local, 36–37; scientists and farmers on, 53–58
Toledo, Victor, 3–4

ABOUT THE AUTHOR

Virginia D. Nazarea is an associate professor of anthropology at the University of Georgia and is director of the Ethnoecology/Biodiversity Laboratory. Before assuming this post, she taught at the Department of Zoology and the College of Human Ecology at the University of the Philippines at Los Banos, and at the Board of Environmental Studies at the University of California at Santa Cruz. She was also a postdoctoral fellow in Social Sciences at the International Potato Center (CIP) and subsequently was assistant director of the User's Perspective with Agricultural and Development (UPWARD). It was while at CIP and UPWARD that Nazarea developed the memory banking approach.

With a background in biology and anthropology, she has focused her research on the interface between the genetic and cultural diversity of crops, particularly on the human cognition, management, and use of plant genetic resources. Her earlier works include an edited volume, *Sweet Potato Cultures of Asia and South Pacific*, a book, *Local Knowledge and Agricultural Decision Making in the Philippines: Class, Gender, and Resistance*, and a review and source book with the International Plant Genetic Resources Institute (IPGRI) and the Food and Agriculture Organization (FAO), *Diveristy in the Shadows: Incorporating Gender Sensitive Approaches into Plant Genetic Resources Use and Conservation*.